The Village Girl Handbook

Volume 2

Persevering Your Way to Maturity

Kristi Burden

Published by Kristi Burden
Nederland, Texas

This book is dedicated in memory of my cousin and best friend, Leah Goates. You faced every struggle head-on with grit and strength. You lent me courage when I needed it and even when I didn't want it. I would gladly have stayed in your shadow, but you wouldn't have that. You left *our village* too soon.

The Village Girl Handbook 2 is dedicated in honor of those in Southeast Texas whose lives have been changed by Hurricane Harvey. To those who watched the waters rising in your homes while waiting for rescue and those who waded in chest-high waters or drove a boat to provide aid for people in need, for those who have given up your bedroom, given a long hug or shared tears over loss, this book is for you. This book is written in honor of those whose homes and cars and sense of normal have been swept under, but still you face each day with determination, strength, and most importantly, hope. Hope in suffering... that's what this book is about.

Table of Contents

Acknowledgements

From Kristi:

My utmost gratitude goes to the author of all good stories (all stories have endless potential when we trust the pen to the creator). How incredibly humbling and empowering it is to have been given the privilege of compiling such wealth into the pages of this book. How utterly exciting it is to be able to share these things with the world in hopes that the world may "*taste and see that (YOU) are good...* (Psalm 34:8)

Thank you story contributors. Emily Ancira, Sheila Bass, Janaye Boyd, Hallie Burden, Rylie Burden, Sara Burt, Ashley Delage, Lily Duong, Gaye Fowler, Crystal Foxworth, Jaime Glenn, Karisa Glenn, Caitlyn Haynes, Denise Hopkins, Jennifer Horner, Rachel Juneau, Amanda Kane, Leigh Karnes, Hailey Kimler, Katie Leavins, Lori Lehrmann, Elizabeth Lott, Jessica Marcantel, Robyn Marriot, Bridget McCarthy, Valerie Morton, Rebecca Mosley, Debbie Nicholson, Emily Neild, Marie Rogers, Vicki Steele, Kelby Stahl, Kaitlyn Sweeney, Taya Tikhova, Leanne Todd, Layla Traweek, Hallie Tyler, Marshaunna Winston, Kirsten and one other special friend whose name isn't mentioned but is nonetheless cherished; you're like a bunch of superheroes in friend clothes. The world will be better for God's work in you and through you. I know my life has been made richer.

You'd never know that I'm technologically, artistically and grammatically challenged. That's because for the past two books I've had a team who makes it look like I know what I'm doing. A special thanks goes to Ruxandra Serbanoiu for the sketches, to Daliborka Mijailovic for the book cover, Sydney Morgan for editing and AAlishaa for formatting. You all did such an outstanding job on the last book that you'll be hardpressed to get rid of me.

Thank you to those who have prayed for *The Village Girl Handbook,* those of you who have bought a copy (or ten) and those of you who have prayed for the ones who will read these books. There aren't beautiful enough words to come up with to give you thanks.

Jason, Hayden, Hallie, and Rylie, you're the perfectly designed grace package. In the eternity I have to figure it out, I doubt I'll ever grasp why God decided to gift me like he has with each of you.

Introduction

Struggle is something that we generally try to avoid. It makes us uncomfortable. Worse, it can leave us feeling defeated and alone. The bad news is we can't entirely avoid struggle.

The good news is, struggle is the very thing that helps us grow and mature in the way God intended. It's often in times of struggle that we find loving community; someone who understands our pain, someone willing to lend a helping hand or a listening ear.

Included in this book are stories and messages written by a host of girls. We've decided to share some of our most private struggles. We want you to know what we've learned. We want you to hear how we overcame. We want you to know that God provides courage and the strength we need. He is faithful to put friends in our lives to remind us that we're never alone. As you hold this book, consider yourself about forty friends richer.

We're wholeheartedly cheering you on even if we haven't met you. Before you decided to read this book we made a choice to be a part of your village. We're now a part of your people, and you're a part of our people.

We've divided this book into five sections we believe are important to your life.

You

In the *You* section, you'll read about some common difficulties (and some unique struggles) girls experience. You'll be reminded of the importance of your character. You'll be encouraged to love yourself and allow yourself room to grow.

Your Hut

This includes the people you live with; your parents and your siblings. *Your Hut* involves people who live under your roof, but also those others that you call family that may live elsewhere. You'll be reminded that families can be complicated but are also one of the best gifts you'll ever be given.

Your Tribe

Your Tribe refers to those who are the same age as you; your peers. This can include your best friend, your acquaintances, and even your mortal enemy. This section gets real and deals with sticky issues like relationship boundaries.

Your Village

A village can be a small living community. We want you to think bigger than that. There are people who may not be your age and are not part of your family, but wholeheartedly *choose* to relate with you and encourage you. They offer you their own stories and they care about yours. This could be a school janitor, a neighbor, the sweet lady at church, or even someone you've read about whom you admire. Pay attention to people who want to show you that life (and God) is good.

Bigger Than That

You were created to love and to be loved. God made you with good plans in mind. You do best when you know and trust the plans he has for you. You'll be reminded that He is always with you. In this section you'll read about all your junk that God wants. He gladly takes our fear, our guilt, our shame, our broken past and creates in us something new and beautiful.

How to go through this book

If you're reading this book alone, make sure you have a pen and a quiet place as your companion. Each story has devotion questions. Fill them out!

This book is also designed so that you can read through it with a mentor or a group. Read through it with your mom, your sister, or a group of friends. Be sure to discuss the questions.

Look for the contributor's name under the title of each story. Each of these stories will have "*Fun Facts*" so that you can get to know each author a bit better outside of her story. The stories without a name and all devotions are written by me, Kristi.

Do you see what this means—all these pioneers who blazed the way, all these veterans cheering us on? It means we'd better get on with it..., start running—and never quit!...
Keep your eyes on Jesus, who both began and finished this race we're in.

Hebrews 1:1-3 (The Message version)

CHAPTER 1

You

You're the only you there is. You're the only you there will ever be. Don't deprive the world by giving up on you or by trying to be someone else. God is equipping you to face the struggles life throws your way. *You* were put here for a reason with a unique style and good plans to accomplish. Be the best you, you can be. The world will be brighter because of it.

Comparing Yourself to Others

Rachel Juneau

Growing up in a competitive family was not so good when your competition was an older brother like mine. He was blessed with charisma, athleticism and oozed talent at everything he tried. My older brother was popular, made good grades without studying and received most of my parents' attention. Life seemed so easy for him.

I never measured up to my brother's success. How could I ever measure up when his walls were filled with trophies and mine were bare? I was obsessed with my deficiencies and participation ribbons. My family always praised his accomplishments, and I felt invisible. I tried everything to get attention, even if it meant receiving punishments for not always making the right choices.

While my brother seemed to breeze through adolescence, I suffered through many years of teenage awkwardness. I was extremely shy and never seemed to fit in. People were always comparing me to my brother, so I struggled with finding my own identity. We were completely different individuals, so it was unreasonable for me to assume we were comparable.

Even though my heart was bursting with jealousy, I looked up to my big brother. I saw his approval directly related to my lovability. If he didn't like me, then how could anyone else? I tried harder and harder, but nothing I did made me feel good enough.

I craved his acceptance so much that I followed in his footsteps and joined the military after high school. I was desperate, and this was one of my last attempts to gain his acceptance. Joining the military built up my confidence, and I learned that I was responsible for my own happiness.

You might not have a sibling who makes you feel inferior, but there might be someone who you admire or make comparisons. They may be more talented, more popular, or have better grades. It is only when you start looking to God for acceptance that you will find your own identity and can focus on your strengths.

Your value comes from the fact that you are made in the image of God. Genesis 1:27 says, *"God created man in his own image; in the image of God he created them."* You possess a soul which has greater value than all the world's riches. God doesn't expect you to be a super athlete, popular, or make straight A's.

He wants your heart, not a trophy.

"For the eyes of the Lord range throughout the earth to strengthen those whose hearts are fully committed to him." 2 Chronicles 16:9

True happiness comes from gaining perspective of yourself from scripture, not from others. There is joy in knowing that God loves you, and He sacrificed Himself for you.

Rachel
Nederland, TX

Fun Facts

1. Kayaking and camping make me happy.
2. I'm a level 31 Pokémon Trainer. Go Team Valor!
3. I will drive hundreds of miles for a good cupcake. My friends call me *The Cupcake Snob.*

"For the eyes of the Lord range throughout the earth to strengthen those whose hearts are fully committed to him." 2 Chronicles 16:9

1. Whose shadow have you felt you lived under at some point in your life?

2. When you feel *in the shadows,* or you start to focus on your weaknesses, how does 2 Chronicles 16:9 say God responds to us?

3. Sometimes we may picture God sitting still on his throne while we suffer or struggle. Is that the picture this verse paints? What is God doing?

Battling Mitochondrial Disease
Emily Neild

I was in the second grade at Regina Howell Elementary when I started to notice something wasn't quite right with my body. I remember telling my mom that my back hurt all day long and that it was hard for me to walk and play at recess.

I went from dancing 4 days a week to not being able to attend my dance classes at all. I was really good at riding a bike and that too quickly changed. It didn't take very long for my friends and teachers to start asking why I didn't feel good and why I looked so skinny.

By the time I made it to 3rd grade I had been hospitalized more than nine times due to a complete failure to thrive, muscle atrophy, and severe constipation. All I really remember about those trips was that I was always in lot of pain, and no one seemed to be able to help me.

It was at this point that my parents thought it would be good for me to go to a private school, Vanguard Classical Academy, where I could attend classes 3 days a week and be home-schooled the other 2 days. This was kind of hard for me to leave all my friends at my other school, but I loved making new friends and getting to meet new teachers!

My 4th-grade year is when my family and I got some answers as to what was going on with me. It was then that I was diagnosed with mitochondrial disease, dysautonomia, hypothyroidism, and no movement (peristaltic) in my large intestine.

The thing about mitochondrial disease is it affects my entire body. I have had multiple procedures and surgeries to help my body do what it once was able to do on its own. I now have a GJ-tube that I get feedings through sometimes, and I have an ileostomy bag to help my intestines work. I have had a ton of upper scopes to diagnose my celiac disease, and tons of scans and ultrasounds to tell me that my thyroid doesn't work anymore and what systems in my body will be affected next.

I have had to learn how to check my own glucose, set up and operate a feeding pump, change my ileostomy bag, and adapt to a new diet for my celiac and mitochondrial disease. I take a bunch of medicine to help my body do what it can't on its own anymore. I often struggle with people knowing that I have an ileostomy bag and have no control over my bodily functions sometimes.

It is also a struggle for me sometimes to do the things that a normal 11-year-old can do, but who likes to be normal all the time anyway! I also really hate when I have to use my wheelchair. I like to think I can do everything on my own, but the truth is sometimes my body needs lots of rest. It's in these hard times that having the help of my family and friends really gets me through.

The rare side to my disease can sometimes make me feel all alone because there are less than 10 people to ever be diagnosed with my kind of mitochondrial disease in the United States. It's a very rare disease to have, but sometimes it's kind of fun to be unique! I have a strong support group in my family and friends. I have lots of really cool doctors that call my momma to talk about me all the time. One of my favorites is my personal nurse Ms. Ashley Atkinson who comes to my house every day to help take care of me. I have a huge church family that prays for me every day, as well as a personal relationship with Jesus Christ who saves me on a daily basis.

My mom tells me that there are many reasons why God chooses someone to live out the calling He places on our lives. Sometimes those callings are tough, and sometimes they are scary. I feel like my purpose is to draw others to know Jesus Christ more. I see how He brings me to the right doctors and hospitals and how He protects me and my family when things are really scary for me.

When those times happen, I pray for God's strength and peace. That always makes me feel better! I know I am stronger with God by my side! I may have to face things on a daily basis that most 11-year-olds do not, but I know in my heart that God has me in the palm of His hands.

Emily
Fearless

Fun Facts:

1. My biggest wish is to attend the Macy's Thanksgiving Parade in New York.
2. I have met Keith Urban and Maddi and Tae (country singers).
3. I am the future president of HB Neild and Son's Construction.

We are pressed on every side, but not crushed, perplexed, but not in despair; persecuted, but not abandoned; struck down, but not destroyed...Therefore we do not lose heart... We fix our eyes not on what is seen, but on what is unseen, since what is seen is temporary, but what is unseen is eternal."
2 Corinthians 4:8-18

1. What do you think would be the most difficult thing about battling a disease like Mitochondrial Disease?

2. What has been your most difficult battle?

3. 2 Corinthians 4 tells us that we find ourselves *pressed, perplexed, persecuted and struck down.* That's the bad news included in living in a broken world. What promise comes with these verses?

We are *not* ____________

We are *not*_____________

We are *not*_____________

We are *not* _____________

Don't Be Afraid to Join the Race
Denise Hopkins

My husband and I went to the auto races to see his close friend, a professional racer, perform that night in the feature race.

In one of the preliminary races, one car at the back of the starting lineup looked totally out of place. The other cars were newly painted, had fresh decals and shiny tires, but this one was beat up, had a dull finish, and its decals were peeling off. It was a real "Junker."

As the cars revved their engines, the flagman started the race and all the cars took off.
As they sped across the line, the race had begun. Then comes "Junker," slowly putt-in' across the starting line. The crowd snickered with some whispering, "Look at him," and "Why is he even here?" As they made their zooming laps, the crowds cheered. And then came "Junker"....putt, putt, putt. The other cars were so fast and skilled that they actually passed a lap around him as the crowd roared with laughter. But he never gave up.

Then things began to happen. One car got a flat tire, another car's motor stalled, and then two cars' bumpers locked in a turn, and on and on until all the other cars dropped out of the race. But what do you know, here comes "Junker," slowly but surely, putt...putt...putt.

As he came into the final lap of the race, the crowd rose to their feet, cheering him on. As he crossed the finish line and the checkered flag fell, the roar and cheers from the crowd were deafening. He actually won! He finished the race, received the grand trophy, a cash prize, and instant notoriety.

Sometimes we want to quit or not even attempt something because we feel unqualified, out-matched, or intimidated. We feel we may not be as "shiny" as someone else or even feel a little "beat up."

You may be trying to share Jesus with a friend, and they don't want to listen.

You may be learning a new skill, such as sewing or cooking, and you just can't get it right.

Do you want to learn a new subject or a talent, like playing a musical instrument, and it seems to be a struggle?

You want to start a new ministry and you're scared.

Don't sit on the sidelines! Enter the race, focus on the goal, and don't quit!

Note: It is sometimes okay to put aside some pursuits when you realize that an idea was really just a whim, or when you realize all your attempts to paint are really a "mess" and not a "masterpiece," or you discover you are not going to be the next music star because you really can't sing.

But other attempts, especially those for God, are worth the rejection, the laughter, the whispers, the struggles, and even the tears.

Now there is not always a trophy, prize, and fame at the end, but do know this…the things we attempt in God's name and His glory will be rewarded by the Father Himself.

Are you going to sit on the sidelines and wonder "what if…?"

Or…are you going to at least try?

I'd rather be a "Junker" and have tried, than to sit on the sidelines and not have tried at all.

Denise

Fun facts:

1. I love any dessert that is chocolate.
2. I love the color RED!!!
3. I cry when anyone else cries.

…You are my servant, Israel, in whom I will be display my splendor…
Isaiah 49:3

1. What do you believe God is calling you to work at using the talents or skills he has gifted you with?

2. What might God be calling you to do that you don't feel is easy for you?

3. How can you give God glory (display his splendor) with the victories you experience and witness?

Dear Future Wives,
Jaime Glenn

It might sound pretty weird to think of yourself as a wife right now. Being married probably seems like a lifetime away. When we look into our future, it is normal to dream about what we hope to become. We think about how great it will be to plan a wedding, graduate from college, receive our first paycheck, or be on our own.

Although it is awesome to think about what we hope to become one day, it is even more important to PRAY about our futures. Pray for God's guidance and direction. When we do this, let's not forget to pray for our one day husband. Yes, as crazy as it sounds praying for a stranger, do it anyway. Pray for your future partner, your future best friend, and your future together as husband and wife.

Trust in the Lord with all your heart, and lean not on your own understanding; in all your ways submit to Him, and He will make your paths straight. Proverbs 3:5

I have been married for over 15 wonderful years. I absolutely adore my husband, and I am grateful that God has united us as one. I have to tell you though, I do not believe, not even for a second, that my husband was a lucky draw. In no way was I fortunate enough to just stumble upon such a great man.

Even now, sometimes I look at him with a full heart and say, "Thank you Lord for preparing him." You see, my husband is an answer to the prayers I prayed when I was younger. I think back now, and I realize that I loved this man even before I knew his name or saw his face.

I remember the day I realized God wanted me to pray for my future husband. I was in junior high, seventh grade, and so ecstatic to be a part of the youth group. My best friend was a year older than me, and she had moved up a whole year earlier. (You can probably imagine how unhappy it made me to stay in the children's group.) Now that I was FINALLY in this group, I wanted to take full advantage of my new found hierarchy. I wanted to participate in everything.

So when my youth pastor suggested we keep a journal and write down our prayers, I was all in. He said that if we saw our heart's desires on paper, we would better understand what was truly important to us. I now know he was talking about perspective and staying focused on what is good.

Finally, brothers and sisters, whatever is true, whatever is noble, whatever is right, whatever is pure, whatever is lovely, whatever is admirable—if anything is excellent or praiseworthy—think about such things. Philippians 4:8

During this time, we journaled but also studied a book. One chapter of this book talked about praying for your future spouse. Keep in mind these prayers are not a wishlist of must-have physical characteristics. You are not writing a letter to Santa Claus predicting your own personal Prince Charming.

When you pray, you are to lift your future husband up to God. Pray for his spiritual growth, his character development, and also your future together as husband and wife. Now if you are a list maker (which I am), here is where your skills will come in handy.

List what a good, faith-based marriage looks like. God knows the desires of your heart, and He wants to fulfill them. Keep in mind though that desires of the heart are not superficial. For example, I prayed for a tall husband, but my husband is just about my height, maybe a tiny bit taller, but God did honor my plea for a loving, compassionate husband who honors his wife and family.

Today I am still praying for my husband. My prayers sound a little bit different though. Now before he goes out the door, I say a prayer for his safety (he's a policeman). I also pray for the safety of his *brothers in blue.* And when he comes home at night and removes his badge and gun, I say a prayer of thanksgiving. Maybe God did not answer ALL my prayers exactly how I asked, but without a doubt, God's plan supersedes the desires of my heart.

For I know the plans I have for you, declares the Lord. Plans to prosper you and not to harm you, plans to give you hope and a future. Jeremiah 29:11

Keep looking up,
Jaime
Praying Girl, Wife, Mother

Fun Facts:

1. Favorite Quote: *Never be afraid to trust an unknown future to a known God.* -Corrie Ten Boom
2. In middle school, I ate cherry sours and Dr. Pepper every day for lunch.
3. When I am scared or nervous about something new, I try to remember, "The scariest moment is always just before you start."

Take delight in the Lord, and he will give you the desires of your heart. Psalm 37:4

1. What does Psalm 37:4 tell us to do for God to give us the desires of our heart?

2. How might the desires of our heart change if we are *delighting in God?*

3. Name 10 (or more) characteristics that you want in a future husband. (Remember to keep those things God values in mind.) These are the things you're hoping for. Then write down five things that you can be praying for him (his safety, that he has good Christian influence in his life…)

What you're hoping for in a spouse:

1.

2.

3.

4.

5.

6.

7.

8.

9.

10.

Five things you're praying for your future spouse:

1.

2.

3.

4.

5.

Anxiety
Katie Leavins

It was the summer after my fifth grade year, and I was at church camp for the first time. The week wasn't going as well as I had hoped, and I was feeling homesick. We were required to play outside for a certain period of time every day, and I could barely stand the heat!

That night, I fell into bed completely exhausted and fell asleep fast. Just a few hours later, my eyes suddenly flew open. I was lying in bed, staring at the ceiling, and feeling afraid. I didn't know why, but I had the feeling something was wrong. My teeth began to chatter, but I wasn't cold. Soon, my whole body was shaking, and I felt my face going numb. I was terrified and thought I was dying!

I jumped down from my top bunk, woke up my best friend, and did my best to explain what was happening. She told me to clench my teeth, but that didn't help. Nothing was helping, and I was growing more and more panicked and unable to breathe. We woke up our sponsor and the two of them walked me down to the nurse's station where I was told I was having a panic attack. It went away after a few minutes and I was okay again, but it was one of the scariest moments of my life.

Over the next few years, I continued to have panic attacks every now and then. They were scary, but they would go away if I got some fresh air, took some deep breaths, and drank some water. On top of the panic attacks, I started having other weird symptoms throughout middle school.

Anytime I would be sitting in class, church, a car, a movie theatre, or any other place where I had to sit and concentrate, I would start to feel like my throat was closing up and I couldn't breathe. I would start to sweat, and my heart would pound. It would go away as soon as I was able to leave the place I was in, so I didn't think much of it or say anything about it. It wasn't until the summer after eighth grade that I realized I had a problem.

I began to have those horrible symptoms more often, almost constantly. My stomach was always in knots and I felt like crying all the time. I ended up going to the doctor and started taking medicine for it. Almost immediately, I felt better and was able to sit in cars, class, and church without feeling like I couldn't breathe. It was the most amazing feeling, and I wondered why I hadn't said anything before.

What I have is called an anxiety disorder. Everyone experiences anxiety every now and then, like when you're about to take a test, perform in a dance recital, or anything else you might get nervous about. That kind of anxiety is normal. However, when it starts to be a constant thing that overwhelms you and keeps you from living your life to the fullest, that's when it becomes a problem. Anxiety disorders can also cause depression; a constant, sad, and empty feeling inside without always knowing why. Depression is when nothing makes you happy anymore, and you don't really feel like getting up in the morning.

I've experienced depression off and on since seventh grade, and it is an awful thing to go through. But, there is hope!

If you think you might have an anxiety disorder or depression, I would encourage you to tell an adult that you trust. Seeing a counselor helps a lot. They are trained to help people who experience these things, and they can give you lots of tips and advice on how to manage it.

If it is bad enough, you might have to go to the doctor. That can be scary. I know I didn't like taking medicine at first, but now I have been taking it for seven years, and I am thankful for it. I believe it is a tool God uses to help us deal with the anxiety and depression.

Don't be afraid to ask for help. Most of all, never, ever lose hope. Reading the book of Psalms helps me a lot when I'm having trouble with my anxiety and depression. A man named David wrote some of that book and, from the sound of it, he struggled with it, too. It's a very hard thing to deal with, but God is always faithful. He sees you, He knows you, and He knows your struggle. He will carry you and be your hope on your darkest days.

Katie
College student

Fun Facts:

1. My friends and I started a girls' ministry when we were in high school. We have a retreat every year for middle school girls where we have worship, Bible study, small group time, games, and just have fun hanging out and learning about Jesus. We love teaching younger girls what we've learned as we've grown up. You can find out more information about it at www.wiwikgirlsministry.com.

2. If I were an animal, I would be a monkey. I like to climb, and I love being out in nature!
3. My favorite Starbucks drink is hot chocolate. I don't like coffee, so I rarely get anything else when I go there, but their hot chocolate is amazing!

Cast all your anxiety on him because he cares for you. 1 Peter 5:7

1. How much of our anxiety is God willing to take?

2. Casting is something you do with a fishing pole. You are placing distance between you and the thing you are *casting.* What worries/fears/anxieties do you need to cast away?

3. Are we just casting our cares upon the water? Where are we casting our anxieties? Why would God want our anxieties?

Separation Anxiety
Kaitlyn Sweeney

As a 4-month-old child, I was taken away from my mom, who had smoking and drinking problems. Just after I turned 3 years old, my dad had a serious industrial accident which left him disabled and with a permanent brain injury. I started living with my loving, and caring grandparents, which I now realize was a gift from God.

Growing up, my grandparents discovered through therapy that I suffered from separation anxiety issues and ADHD. In the mornings after I woke, I would go check to make sure they were still alive and ok. I was scared I was going to lose them and have nobody. Unlike many other kids, I would not go outside by myself or even down the hall to my room. Every step I took I made sure my grandparents were right there watching. Because of this, I was shy and it was hard to make good friends.

Getting involved in church helped me in every way. I gained many good friends there. I was taught that when my grandparents weren't there, Jesus was! And He was ready to take super good care of me. I had a fear of being alone, but I realized through church that you are not. God is with you. He is right by your side and is never leaving. No one can separate you from God! He's there eternally. Hearing this, I started walking to my room all by myself and even going outside to play.

The first time I went to GA (Girls in Action) camp with my church, I can't explain enough how thankful I was for the mothers that went. It helped me feel more secure having them there and their cell phones so I could call home every single night. Each year I went, it got easier and easier for me. Doing these things helped me with my anxiety because I knew that the people I was around loved and cared about me as much as my grandparents did. I felt like I belonged there.

Church is a second home and family for me. Every Sunday since I was itty bitty, during the time of greeting I have gone around and hugged as many people as I can. It gives me so much joy to give love and receive it. This means so much because you don't know what another person is going through. It could be the only hug they receive that week.

Just remember you are not alone. You have God and all your new friends from this book. There is always a place you will be received, loved and feel safe. You may have to search, but never give up! You have a place in God's Kingdom. Make Him your home!

Kaitlyn
Nederland, TX
10th-grade student

Fun Facts:

1. There are two under-bed trays filled with every stuffed animal I had since my birth.
2. Every night before I go to bed I touch or move everything I own that's visible. I don't know why but I must do it.
3. I'm one of those people that might take a French fry off your plate even though I have a whole plate of them. Sorry I just can't help myself. Lol!

I give them eternal life, and they will never perish, and no one will snatch them out of my hand. John 10:28 (ESV).

1. What does Kaitlyn say her fear was?

2. Why do you believe Kaitlyn getting involved in church helped her with her separation anxiety?

3. Where does John 10 say believers are kept?

Being THAT Kid
Rylie Burden

Being the pastor's daughter is challenging. People think *that I think* I'm better than them because my dad is the person wearing the velvety black suit and tie; the person who speaks with confidence. My mom shows up in her weekly necklace with a warm smile and caring hug. I'm proud to be there. I try and greet as many people as possible during greeting time before I have to crawl back into my pew.

It's not all cupcakes and gumdrops. When I raise my hand in school and church, it's thought that I'm bragging about what I know. When I'm being nice to someone or deciding not to do something that could get me into trouble, I'm considered a goody-two-shoes. If I disagree with someone and let them know, I'm reminded that I'm *supposed to be the pastor's daughter...perfect.*

Obviously, since I've been taught right from wrong and my father is the pastor, I shouldn't do anything wrong. I'm not just a kid living out my life, like the others who get to judge me. I'm the pastor's daughter rather than the kid who gets to make mistakes. Or at least that's what has been implied my entire life.

A dentist wants his kids to have pearly-white, healthy teeth. He probably checks their teeth frequently and takes care of any problem they have, just like my parents make sure I'm growing in my relationship with God. Still, I don't think anybody asks a dentist's kid if their dad "knows they've been eating candy." Dentists' kids don't get tattled on when someone finds out they haven't been flossing.

There are a sliver of people who see me as Rylie. They see me as a "Plain Jane," no one whose actions are any more important, someone they consider a friend. I can joke with them. I can laugh with them when their mustard packet busts and mustard flies across the table, without being judged. Those are the people I choose to spend my time with.

I worry when I have a disagreement with my friends because I don't want to lose the few friends who have accepted me as I am. In the end, they don't use my insecurity, me trying to be acceptable, against me. They're just good old "Plain Janes" like me.

I've figured out everybody is a "Plain Jane" with their quirks and insecurities. At some point in life, they're held up to high expectations that others set for them. They listen to people telling them *this is who you need to be.* Most people fail at becoming who everyone else thinks they should become, but in the end, even the people who meet those high expectations others set aren't always the happiest. They hide their weaknesses to try and *keep* others' approval.

- Realize you're not perfect. Let your flaws show.
- Don't listen to people who care more about what you do or don't do than they care about you as a person.
- Know that you have a purpose that *God* gave you. Seek it.

- Don't change who you are by trying to live the purpose someone else has decided for you.
- Don't correct others unless they know you care about them as a person.

Rylie

Fun Facts:

1. I keep plastic cards (kind of like credit cards) to scratch my legs and arms. I have a Mast Cell Disorder that makes me itch like crazy.
2. I made my first wedding cake at age 10.
3. When I was younger, I had a reputation for asking for strange gifts like a Geico robot, a taxi cab, and a Life Alert necklace.

The Spirit himself testifies with our spirit that we are God's children...
Romans 8:16

1. In what ways have you felt people tried to define who you are? Have you been defined as *the smart girl, the goody two shoes, the bad girl, the athletic one, the teacher's kid, the suck up...?*

2. Have you been guilty of defining others, boxing them in, while forgetting that we're all *fearfully and wonderfully made* creatures who make mistakes?

3. According to Romans 8:16, for those of us who trust in Christ, who does the Spirit of God say we are? What can we do to get better about listening to the Spirit rather than those around us?

Pray, asking that God will remind you who you are when others try to make you doubt your worth.

Forgiveness
Hallie Burden

I can say without a doubt that granting forgiveness is one of the hardest things you will ever have to do. It can seem so much easier to hold on to anger and hatred because you feel like that is what the person who hurt you deserves. I found myself in this situation at a time where I was in a very dark, vulnerable place.

I was in a bad relationship. It seemed like I had nobody to confide in. I finally found a friend who I felt like I could talk to about all the chaos in my life. I thought I found someone because this person was willing to listen to all the dark and messy parts of my life and be with me regardless.

But they didn't stick around. They left in the worst way possible. The person I confided in (and a person I had been friends with for years) walked out of my life forever in a matter of minutes because I didn't do exactly as they thought I should.

And they didn't just leave. Leaving me at my lowest wasn't enough, they betrayed my trust and told people I barely knew secrets I told only them. They told lies about me. They called me names and made me feel the lowest I'd ever felt, even in the dark, vulnerable place I was already in.

I was angry. I hated them. I told myself I would never forgive them.

But the thing is, they didn't care. They didn't want my forgiveness. The anger and hatred I had towards them was only affecting me. I had to let go and forgive.

It was hard to forgive someone who wasn't even sorry. It was hard to forgive someone who I didn't even think deserved my forgiveness. But that wasn't my decision to make. Only God can decide who deserves forgiveness. I didn't forgive them just for their sake, I also did it for mine. Once I forgave them, the joy they once stole from me was returned. I could move on with life. When I was holding on to anger, what they did to me hurt me every day that I hadn't forgiven them.

Forgiveness took a lot of time along with effort and prayer. I had to pray a lot and make a conscious decision that I was going to forgive them *and stick with it.* Although it was one of the hardest decisions I've ever made I know it was for the best.

I honestly believe it would have been harder to have to be angry every single day. If there is someone in your life who hurt you or walked out, forgive them. We don't get to decide who does and doesn't deserve forgiveness. But you don't forgive because you feel like they deserve it. You forgive because you deserve to be free; to not be plagued by constant anger when their name comes to mind or when you see their face.

Although you won't forget what they did to you, you'll learn from it and even grow from it, so strong that what they did will never hurt you again.

A Now Stronger
Hallie

Fun Facts:

1. When I started growing hair on my legs, I thought I was turning into a horse.
2. At 4 years old I could sing the entire soundtrack of Phantom of the Opera.
3. In kindergarten I had to sit out from recess, and my mom had to meet with all the teachers because I was using inappropriate karate moves.

Bear with each other and forgive one another if any of you has a grievance against someone. Forgive as the Lord forgave you. Colossians 3:13

1. When have you apologized for something you did wrong?

2. Do you forgive easily when someone apologizes? What about when they don't? Read Colossians 3:13 again. Does it say we should forgive even if someone hasn't asked?

3. Why does this verse say we should forgive?

About Those Selfies

You walked into the party
Like you were walking onto a yacht
Your hat strategically dipped below one eye
Your scarf, it was apricot
You had one eye on the mirror...

You're So Vain-Carly Simon

I have a friend who could write the book on selfies. She knows about angles, filters and natural light. If you were her friend on Instagram, you'd know she's pretty proud of her selfies, even the old "duck face" ones that you'd have to scroll back a year to see. I think those are old school now, thank goodness. They've been replaced with the "fish gape" face, which isn't much better (in my humble selfie opinion).

Not long ago I watched someone sitting on the edge of a couch trying to capture the perfect selfie. She was having a little trouble. What I observed was a pattern. She would cock her head, just so, flashing a brilliant smile, and then she'd click. Then she'd check her selfie and grimace, unsatisfied. Then she'd repeat. She grew disturbed. The funny thing is, she pretty much kept doing the same thing, but couldn't understand why the results were the same (...doing the same thing and expecting different results...Isn't that the definition of insanity or something?).

When I was in junior high and high school I hid from the camera, even if I was wearing my favorite shirt, had spent two hours mastering my hairdo, and the cameraman had given me ample time to get my "cheese" grin ready (do people still even say *cheese* for pictures?).

What I do know is that both *selfie stars, perceived selfie failures* and *trained camera avoiders* can be overly obsessed with:

-The way they look
-The way they perceive others feel about how they look

- The constant thinking that you look good and the desire for other people to have the opportunity to be reminded that you look good is unhealthy (take that, selfie queens).
- The overthinking on your appearance (to the point of having a complex), that you aren't pretty enough/thin enough/photogenic enough is unhealthy.

Where did we get the idea that our appearance (and people's thoughts on it) is of such importance?

Yeah, I know. The world tells us. But I thought we were smarter than that. *The world lies.*

It tries to convince us to be consumed by our own beauty. Then we can spend money and time trying to uphold a beauty standard based on cosmetics, the right clothes and a perfect pose. The world tries to make us believe that we're not beautiful. We wallow in self-pity and can become jealous or critical of those around us who we think meet the beauty standard the world has set. We see what we consider lacking in our own appearance and then search for what is lacking in others.

What a waste of time.

In our obsession, we're distracted from all the beauty that God has designed to be *in* us like purity and unselfishness. When we focus on our *looks,* we're distracted from the beauty he's placed around us in sunrises, and in people beating cancer, and through a weed that (against the odds) pushes its way through the sidewalk.

Yes, you're beautiful. Get past that. Beauty is all around you. Appreciate it in yourself and search for it abroad. Capture it. Release it. Create it.

Your beauty should not come from outward adornment, such as elaborate hairstyles and the wearing of gold jewelry or fine clothes {or selfies thereof}. Rather, it should be that of your inner self, the unfading beauty of a gentle and quiet spirit, which is of great worth in God's sight.
1 Peter 3:3-4

1. How have you been guilty of behaving like a selfie queen?

2. How are you guilty of tearing yourself down concerning your image?

3. Rather than focusing on our outward appearance (or the appearance of others), what inner characteristics does God deem valuable? What do you think a gentle and quiet spirit looks like?

Half Baked Pies (and Ideas)

My summers growing up consisted of bike rides and impulsive genius ideas. Many of these adventures included my cousin Leah who'd moved to Iredell (my town) her fourth-grade year. We'd meet up at Granny's house where we could find a little more to get into.

One afternoon we decided to bake apple pies. Why not? Leah had an Easy Bake oven. This *magic machine* came with tiny pie pans and a kit that made crusts. We found some apples and a butter knife. Granny left us alone in the kitchen to *do our thing.* In no time we had half a dozen little pieces of heaven, or so we thought. They looked just like delicious pie (on the outside).

We decided to grace the neighborhood, selling each small pie for fifty cents. Our first customer bought two! Quickly thereafter we sold three of the four remaining delectable desserts. We saved one for later for ourselves.

Having no desire to experience summer day boredom, we went back and grabbed our bikes. We took a shady street to avoid the midday heat; the same street where customer number one bought two of our pies. To our dismay, we spied this same lady feeding the fruits of our labor...*to her horses.* We jumped off our bikes and watched in horror through the fence.

We were puzzled. How could she throw out our baked masterpieces?

While cooking our pies we were careful to make sure the crust was light brown on top. We'd even used a fork to crimp the outer edges. Those pies looked pretty fancy. Deciding we'd better try our pie, we made a quick cut into it. As the fork made effort to cut through the apples we heard a soft crunch. We diagnosed the problem. The apples weren't done.

Our pie was half-baked.

I've grown up now (in many ways). I no longer make half-baked pies, but I have plenty of half-baked ideas. I mean, many of the decisions I make aren't *fully thought out.* I forget to think before I speak...or act.

We would have done well to have followed good directions when baking our pies. We would have been wise to have tested them before we served them up. For our thoughts to be fully-cooked and our behaviors to be considered well-done, proper time must be spent with God. It's necessary that we pay attention to the directions He gives us in His word. We need to consider, in prayer, what He says is good. We need to *think* on Him.

When I think on my ways, I turn my feet to your testimonies. Psalm 119:59 (ESV)

How many of the following half-baked ideas have you tried? How many half-cooked behaviors have you served up? Of which of the following are you guilty?

___Participating in gossip

___Cheating

___Lying

___Trying to make someone jealous

___Caring too much about your physical appearance/Caring too much about someone else's

___Being critical/judgmental of yourself or someone else

___Carrying shame

___Choosing bad company

___Using inappropriate language

___Watching/listening to something you shouldn't (on the radio, TV or a handheld device like a tablet)

___Posting something inappropriate on social media

___Snapping at your parents or someone else

___Behaving selfishly

So prepare your minds for action and exercise self-control. Put all your hope in the gracious salvation that will come to you when Jesus Christ is revealed to the world.
1 Peter 1:13 (NLT)

1. How can you *prepare your mind* to make good decisions? (What has God provided to help you out?)

2. When it comes to self-control, you should be aware of bad behaviors you're tempted to display? What are some of those?

3. What, or who, should our hope be fixed on so that our thoughts (and then actions) will be fully-cooked/well made?

Instead of following through with half-baked ideas, ask yourself:

Does the thing I'm about to do or say dishonor God? If it does, don't say it or do it.

Sometimes we don't know the answer to that question. Always remember to seek God's help by praying and reading His word. God shares all the ingredients for a *good life.*

CHAPTER 2

Your Hut

Just like you're an individual, your family is unique. You won't look like anyone else's family. Not all families consist of a dad, a mom, a brother, a sister and a cute dog named Spot. Families aren't perfect. Even families of five with the cute dog must work together to smooth the rough edges and work through problems. Learning to love and support the family you've been given will make for a better you and a better family.

Being an Only Child
Amanda Kane

Growing up as an only child, I felt like I was truly missing out on something. Family functions were small and dinnertime was low key (even though we always ate together). I'd hear or see my friends with their big families and siblings and was curious what that was like. I wondered if it was something I would long for and miss for the rest of my life.

Don't get me wrong. Back to school shopping and Christmas, or the like, was fabulous as I was the sole benefactor, ha ha! But still, was I missing out on a cherished relationship with a person that would be there no matter what for the rest of my life? Well – maybe… maybe not…

I craved a solid friendship bond between my girlfriends, like the one I thought sisters would share – even though I may not have realized that's what I wanted at the time. In junior high and high school, finding that true lasting relationship is HARD! What feels real one minute, you learn, isn't the next. It felt like friends and BFF's shuffled week to week.

In short I would pull away from friendships with girls, or at least the ones fighting for popularity constantly, and found it easier to talk to the boys. The ups and downs of those relationships didn't appeal to me, and I didn't understand. Maybe boys were easier to talk to, or maybe there were fewer hormones to combat. Even in college one of my best friends was a guy – the thought of a romantic relationship never crossed my mind because, *ewww, he was like my brother!*

Fast forward to my 'grown up' life… I've learned so much more about myself and what types of relationships I have with people. I truly have a diverse group of friends that all support and love me in different ways. I still keep in touch with a few of my high school/college friends, but I also now have a fabulous group of women I can lean on in my daily life.

Do I have a spiritual struggle, experienced mom question, or do I just need to vent and have coffee or tacos with someone who will listen and not judge?! Lucky for me I have friends that serve all those needs and then some! I have a TRIBE, and they are all amazing!! I feel like my relationships are far better than what I imagined in having a sibling. It might be hard for some people to understand, but blood doesn't always make a family...at least in my experience!

Amanda
from Texas

Fun Facts:

1. When I was in elementary and middle school, I loved using coffee-mate instead of milk in my cereal for breakfast.
2. I was a math nerd from an early age – I always managed the money at our family garage sales. And I remember learning about annu-

ities in high school and thought that was the coolest thing ever!

3. In junior high I was blessed to be a part of an amazing youth group where we would get together weekly for Bible study, events like 5th quarter after football games, but also would have impromptu hang outs that allowed for candid discussions and learning. I certainly had exposure to my church as a child, but it was through this group that I was able to truly learn what it meant to accept Jesus and become a Christian. The youth group leader and my friends helped start my journey and relationship with God, and I am grateful for their role in that.

Love wisdom like a sister; make insight a beloved member of your family. Proverbs 7:4 (NLT)

1. As a child what did Amanda believe was missing?

2. Who filled that void?

3. What does Proverbs 7:4 compare wisdom to? What about insight (understanding)? In what ways did God add to Amanda's family?

Losing a Parent
Karisa Glenn

I remember the day she left for the hospital for a minor surgery. My mom told me "*Goodbye*" and that she would see me the next day. I went to school that morning, and life appeared normal.

By the next morning, life was anything but normal. My mother had developed a complication after surgery, and we would shortly be saying our final goodbye.

I lost my mother to a sudden illness when she was just 31 years of age. I was the oldest of 4 children when this happened. I was 11 years old. I can feel the lump in my throat to this day, and my heart aches knowing I will never see her on this Earth again.

Having to grow up without a mother was just one of the many hardships of being a child, or a girl rather. As children we look up to our parents, grandparents, or whomever assumes the responsibility of raising us. We typically don't find ourselves imagining they won't be there for us tomorrow.

When this happens, we have to lean on God for understanding, guidance, hope, love and faith in knowing that we will see our loved ones again someday. We will never again live on this Earth together, but if we chose to accept Jesus into our hearts and lives, then we will live together again in Heaven one day.

If I had to devise a plan for my life, or the life of any child, I would never choose for them or myself to grow up without their mother or parent. Ultimately though, I don't get to choose all of the details of my life or any others, God has control over all of that.

I don't believe that God puts these challenges or obstacles in our lives to make life difficult or unpleasant. I believe God allows these things in our lives to make us the people He desires us to be. God does not want us to be sad, depressed or angry at Him, but rather He wants us to lean on Him and to have faith that everything will work out the way it should, and that He will receive all of the glory.

God loves us and wants all of His children to be loved by their parents, grandparents or whomever raises us. If we find ourselves in a life where we don't have Earthly parents, we should rest assured that we have a Father in heaven who loves us so much He sent His only son for us.

Karisa
Kindergarten Teacher
Waxahachie, Texas
Wife and mother of 4

Fun Facts:

1. I barrel raced as a teen, which was interesting because I'm aller-

gic to horses.

2. I sprained my right wrist really badly in the fifth grade, and cheer tryouts were the following week. I had to try out using one arm including doing one-armed cartwheels...I made cheerleader though.
3. I grew up hunting squirrels, deer, and ducks with my daddy. Some of the best memories were those hunting adventures.

He heals the brokenhearted and binds up their wounds. Psalm 147:3

1. Does the Bible promise that if we trust in Him we'll never be wounded? What does He say He will do for our wounds?

2. Why does Karisa say God allows suffering? Will our suffering and

sorrow last forever?

3. Binding up wounds is similar to wrapping a hurt ankle or bandaging a cut. One must be close and present to bind wounds. What does this mean about where God is when we're brokenhearted and injured?

The Party
(On Rejection)
Part 1 - Ashley Delage

My birthday was in February, which in our area is one of the coldest months. My sister Brett was 11 years younger than me, and my parents never let me have a lot of people over for my parties. My birthday parties were usually only a few friends and mostly family (since I came from such a large one). But on this occasion, I wanted just a *friends only* party, no family!

After much convincing, my parents finally let me have a dance party for my 13th birthday! We agreed that my sister Brett was not going to be there, because who wants their 2-year-old sister around. The party would be from 6pm-8pm, and I could invite around 20 girls.

Two weeks before my party, I started to hand out the invites to a few of my classmates. Everyone seemed to really be excited and most were coming, from what they had told me! As each day passed, my mom had gotten everything ready: pizza, music from my Aunt Becca, and a cookie cake!

When the day finally came, I couldn't contain my excitement! I sat outside waiting on friends to arrive about 30 minutes before the party was to begin. As the minutes passed it had gotten dark outside, and I went inside to see if anyone had called. I remember seeing the sadness in my mom's eyes as she told me no, so there I sat waiting for anyone to walk through that door.

Around 7:30 the doorbell rang, and I ran to the door to see my friend Meagan! To say I was excited would be an understatement, but that shortly passed as she told me that she wasn't able to stay long. I made the most of the short time she was there. We danced, listened to Hanson (the best boy band at the time) and cut into that delicious cookie cake!

Finally, I asked her why she couldn't stay longer, and that's when I knew why no one came that night. A girl in my class decided to have an indoor swimming party the same night, and everyone was there. Unfortunately I was not invited, and to this day I'm not sure why. Meagan left about 30 minutes after she had gotten there. My heart was broken!

Ashley
Mother of 2

Fun Facts:

1. I didn't start my period until I was a junior in high school.
2. I love anything Disney!
3. A little over a year ago I would have never opened a Bible, let alone understood anything I read out of it, until my friend helped me learn more.

The After Party
Part 2-Written by Ashley's Mom (Debbie Nicholson)

The look on Ashley's face would kill any mother. She felt alone, dejected and embarrassed. I wanted to fix the problem, so I called her Aunt Becca and told her what happened.

About 15 minutes later, the doorbell rang. Ashley ran to the door as she rubbed her eyes. She opened the door and Becca and Brett walked in. Becca said that Brett was ready to come home, so she brought her home. Ashley laughed because Brett never stayed with anyone. It was a good cover. She never suspected that I called her aunt. Becca was her "cool aunt. " Becca and Ashley listened to music, ate and laughed. When the party was over, Becca asked Ashley and I if we wanted to go for a little ride.

The back seat of her car was packed with rolls of toilet paper, bags of colorful confetti, and plastic forks. Becca said that it was about time that Ashley wrap a house. It is a sign that you are a grown up when you successfully wrap a house without them knowing who did it. We drove around trying to find the perfect house. We stopped in front of Allen and Andrea's house. They had just moved there, and Ashley hadn't seen the house yet. Becca said that we had to be quiet.

She showed Ashley how to throw the rolls of toilet paper so that it goes up and wraps around a tree limb. It took a few tries, but Ashley got the hang of it. We started to put plastic forks in the ground when the porch light came on and the door started to open. Becca told Ashley to run and get in the car. As we were running to the car, a man's voice yelled at us. Ashley was scared that we were in trouble. When no one followed us, Becca told Ashley that she successfully wrapped a house. Ashley said, "That means I'm not a little kid anymore, and I'm all grown up." Ashley laughed the whole way home and told Becca that this was her best birthday.

Aunt Becca saved her birthday. When I called her, she had made arrangements with Andrea and Allen to let Ashley wrap their house. Allen even told Becca that he would scare us. Becca and I went back the next day and cleaned it up. I thanked Becca for everything she did. Ashley bragged to her friends about what happened at her party. She never mentioned that no one showed up.

It was family she didn't want at her party, but it was her aunt that gave her the best birthday ever. Ashley learned so much on that important birthday.

Family is important.
Friends love to swim, even in February.

Ashley's 13th birthday didn't leave any scars. Her next birthday was a total success. And later, just as Aunt Becca saved her birthday, Ashley came to her little sister Brett's rescue on her birthday fiasco.

Debbie (Ashley's Mom)

What then shall we say in response to these things? If God is for us, who can be against us? Romans 8:31

1. In the Bible, Romans 8:31 is in a section titled *More than Conquerors.* How did Ashley's family help her conquer her birthday disaster? Write down a time a family member went out of their way to help you through a tough time.

2. Has there been a time that your family tried to *fix* a difficult situation or *encourage you,* but they had little power to make things better? Has there been a difficult situation where your family couldn't be there? What was it?

3. God is in control of all things. How is this different from your family? God is ever-present. He is not only always *for* you, He is always *with* you. How is this different from your favorite people on the planet?

Thank God for giving you a family that loves you deeply and works hard to provide a good and happy life for you. Thank God that He is *for you* and *with you* in ways that a family wants to be but can't.

#appreciate
Robyn Marriot

When I was in the 8th grade, my parents told me that for the remainder of my school years my sisters and I would be homeschooled. This was most definitely NOT preferred. I was looking forward to public high school with sports and events and activities and new friends. This was a serious blow in the life of an early teen, so my attitude about the whole thing really kind of stank.

My family owned an electrical business, and our shop had a huge upstairs room for storage. My mom worked her tail off to transform that space into a full-fledged classroom. I mean, the woman went all out.

She bought desks for us and her, a chalkboard, books and bookshelves, and even classroom decorations, complete with a life-size map of the entire world. She poured over curriculums every night, trying to decide which one would be best. Should she use this Math book or that English book? And don't get me started on the Bible classes…

You know what? My ninth grade year actually wasn't that bad after all.

The thing that I didn't realize until later on, however, was that my parents actually weren't trying to ruin life as I knew it as a teenager. They made the decision for our family, and they felt like it was the absolute best direction, God's direction, for our lives.

The countless hours of prayer that went into it probably made angels sing! And yet I completely took for granted the fact that they not only wanted to do the right thing for us, but they also wanted to make it as smooth as possible, knowing it would be a tough "family move."

Looking back, I sincerely appreciate them for making an unpopular decision, dealing with 3 girls and their attitudes, and still bending over backwards to make it work with as little discomfort as possible!

Recognize the people in your life who truly want what is best for you, and show them the appreciation they deserve!

Robyn
Joshua, Texas

Fun Facts:

1. When cliff-jumping at Lake Whitney a couple years ago, I somehow hit the water sideways and broke 3 ribs. One of them punctured my left lung, and they had to install a chest tube so it wouldn't collapse!
2. I LOVE watching sports, but baseball is my absolute favorite. GO TEXAS RANGERS!
3. I've been married for 15 years to the man of my dreams. He brought a little overall-wearing blonde 3-year-old with him to the party, and since then we have had 3 more boys. 4 boys total! Let me tell you about my grocery bill…

Commit to the Lord whatever you do, and he will establish your plans.
Proverbs 16:3

1. What did Robyn's mom do in spite of Robyn's attitude about being homeschooled?

2. How did Robyn's attitude change?

3. Robyn suggests that her mother put in *countless hours of prayer* along with the work that she did in preparing to homeschool her girls. How was Robyn's mom following Proverbs 16:3? What was the outcome?

Birth Order
Three Sisters (Vicki, Kristi and Jennifer)

The Oldest (Vicki)

I am the oldest sister. I paved the highway for my two younger sisters. I'm the barrier breaker. The responsibility queen. The cook. The maid. The taxi driver. The leader without ever losing my cool factor.

I was the first to experience every rite of passage including *puberty, the first kiss, marriage and becoming a mother.* I'm the book of knowledge openly sharing the *ups and downs.* With my help, my sisters learned how to make everything from a French braid to smothered steak.

Parents are hardest on the oldest. I had to wear a dress every week to school, and I couldn't tuck my pants in my boots. Those rules were long gone by the time *the babies* came along. I had way more responsibilities than my sisters. I cooked, cleaned and washed the family's clothes while the girls watched *Gilligan's Island* and *My Little Pony* and dropped Little Debbie crumbs all over the couch and floor (sorry... got a little sidetracked.).

When it came to boyfriend issues, I didn't have that older sister there to confide in or walk me through. I was the secret keeper without having a sister old enough to share my secrets with.

Being the oldest felt like a hardship at the time, but now I can see how the extra responsibility prepared me for who I was to become. A neat freak. A leader. A good friend and listener.

I still find myself taking charge and giving advice when I spend time with my sisters. The playing field has become even. I now have someone that I can share my secrets with. There is no better friend than a sister.

The Middle (Kristi)

The other day while perusing the office supply aisle in Target, I saw a pair of ceramic pineapple bookends. I thought about buying them even though I really didn't have a need for them. In a grouping of books, those *shiny things* would stand out. Growing up I saw my sisters (and my older brother who was about the same age as my older sister) as the eye-catching bookends. Me? I was the *middle thing*. Filler.

I once allowed a family member to shock my foot with a *Snake Doctor* (a novel gadget of the late 80's which was intended to deliver 25,000 volts of electricity to victims of snake bites). Nobody else in the family volunteered, so I saw it as my moment to shine. No pain? No glory.

I'm not the oldest, the one we've looked up to. Being a girl who looked up to her older sister, if she wore it, I'd wear it with confidence (even if it didn't fit). If she said it, I believed it. I sought her advice on makeup and boys.

The baby was the one we always thought was the cutest, our favorite toy. That wasn't me.

I was never quite as adorable as my little sister who we'd encourage to do *Gremlin* and *Cowardly Lion* impersonations and who I begged to let me do her hair.

I imagined myself less fun or awe-inspiring.

My older sister had barely left for college when I attempted to wear the prized *Older Sister Badge.* I threw out sage advice for my younger sister and made the contents of my closet available to her. Whereas I once sought the attention of my older sister, my new endeavor was to seek the acceptance of my younger sister. Unfortunately I still wasn't the older sister but rather the *younger* older sister to the independent baby.

And then we grew. The caricature version of each of us softened. My cool older sister stayed cool, and the little sister has kept life thrilling. I'm sure I add something to the mix, but I've grown secure enough not to focus too much on what that is. It's no longer a competition where there are distinct places, or not that I care to notice. We complement one another. And I like to be *in the middle* of that.

The Baby (Jennifer)

What can I say, the rubber stamp says the youngest is spoiled, charming, a wild child, fun loving, and irresponsible. While some of that may be true, here's the lowdown on being *the baby* of the family.

We have it made! End of story. Parents are too tired and don't sweat the small stuff by the time *us babies* are born. We have older siblings who will let us hang with them and sleep in their room. They'll tell you about life; explain things you're too afraid to ask your parents about. You get to borrow their stuff and get help on homework. It's awesome being the *baby*!

Brake Check! (Aka reality check!) Here's the rest of the story. As the youngest child I spent a lot of time playing by myself while they went to school, went on dates, and hung out with friends. I got bossed around, laughed at, and literally carried off from a social gathering over a sibling's shoulder. My siblings never forgot the dumb/evil things I did; yet, I was too young (or too inattentive) to remember any dirt on them.

I got left behind as they got married, went to college, and started families of their own. The worst of it was when I saw my siblings get hurt, being too young to even offer them advice (not having experienced life myself) I got to watch them hurt instead.

So there it is, the essence of being the *baby* of the family. Stamp us as being spoiled, charming, wild, fun loving, and irresponsible. OK … but we are also empathetic, because we hurt before we experienced it. We are intelligent, able to learn from the mistakes of others. We are also independent because they eventually move away. We are tough because we had to be. *Us babies* embrace life and go with the flow because the path was paved before us, and we have an idea of what's ahead.

We didn't ask for this position in the family, but we are smart enough to take advantage of what life hands us by being the last child.

To be honest I love being the baby! They'll always be older and I get to watch them become crazy, senile old toots, giving me the last laugh!

Vicki Steele
Kristi Burden
Jennifer Horner

Fun Sister Facts:

1. We came in "5's". First came Vicki. Five years and two days later came Kristi. And in five more years came Jennifer.
2. We have an older brother David who we probably wore out as he took it upon himself to be our protector. We kind of appreciate it now.
3. Between us we've added four in-laws and thirteen grandkids and two greats to the mix (with one on the way) making for loud and crazy family get-togethers.

Two are better than one, because they have a good reward for their toil. For if they fall, one will lift up his fellow. But woe to him who is alone when he falls and has not another to lift him up. Ecclesiastes 4:9-10 (ESV)

1. Each sister felt there was a disadvantage to the *order of their birth.* Can you relate to any of the *complaints* they mentioned?

2. Do you believe God has a particular purpose for the way he orders us in families? Is there purpose in being the oldest? The middle? The youngest? An only child? A twin?

3. What is a benefit of having a sibling?

Convicted to Love
Gaye Fowler

Have you ever felt isolated, apart from the crowd? You don't fit in! You don't see eye to eye with your peers. Differences in standards and beliefs can put you at odds with others, and you can become the target of criticism for not conforming to this world's acceptance of things that we believe are wrong.

My parents and grandparents were very conservative and strict. It would take a page to list the "do nots". The do list was simple and short. Go to church, read your Bible, pray, and *"Love your neighbor as yourself."* As I grew up, being accepted among my peers was relatively easy as many of the kids in my school had pretty much the same rules. I was not exposed to alcohol nor tobacco except a grandfather that mostly smoked a pipe.

Then I came face to face with one of my major upbringing no no's, alcohol! I now had an alcoholic in my family who was verbally and emotionally abusive. He knew I was brought up in a home that regularly went to church and was against alcohol. He considered me a "goody two shoes."

I could not accept his drinking, and he had problems with my non-acceptance of his drinking. I didn't want my children to be exposed to alcohol. I wanted them to grow up in an environment that fit my way of thinking, my beliefs, and my values. It was unacceptable. I wanted a perfect world for my family.

I couldn't change him and I could not change my values nor my beliefs. What could I do? I could change my attitude and the way that I perceived him. I could accept him as a human with frailties, and imperfections. We all are frail with imperfections and sins. *"For all have sinned and fall short of the glory of God"* (Romans 3:23). I wouldn't change my values, but I would be more compassionate and accept him in love.

In the time I spent with him, we began to see each other in a new light. I became one of his favorites. He even gave me his prize possession. His drinking and smoking finally took its toll on his life. Cirrhosis of the liver from drinking and emphysema from smoking were killing him. I visited him in the hospital and prayed for his physical and spiritual being. On one of my visits he told me that everything was ok. He didn't need the pamphlets on *how to be saved* anymore. He was a new person.

His last request of me, the day before he died, was to make him some Indian moccasins. Not knowing that this would be the last time that I would see him, I felt the urge to make the moccasins, finishing them on my way to see him. Only hours after I left, he went home wearing his new moccasins.

This world is filled with discord. Be steadfast in your beliefs. Be strong and not swayed by the world, but be forgiving when you are accused of having hate. What can you do when you are persecuted for your beliefs? Be patient, be kind, be loving, be caring. Most of all lift them up in your prayers.

Blessed is the man who remains steadfast under trial, for when he has stood the test he will receive the crown of life, which God has promised to those who love him. James 1:12 (ESV)

Fun Facts:

1. I grew up in Early, Texas, near the Pecan Bayou where we fished. We had a garden, along with horses, chickens, and dogs. My brother named the chickens Friend Harmon, Hunk of Cheese, She Pigeon By Known, and other quirky names.
2. My cousin was the closest that I came to having a sister.
3. My husband and I have been married 50 years. We have 4 children, 13 grandchildren and 3 great-grandchildren.

But the wisdom that comes from heaven is first of all pure; then peace-loving, considerate, submissive, full of mercy and good fruit, impartial and sincere. James 3:17

1. What sinful behavior is difficult for you to be around? When around someone who behaves in that sinful manner, what is your response? Do you confront them and tell them why their behavior is wrong? Avoid them? Overlook their behavior? Is there a time for each of these responses?

2. What are the 8 specific characteristics of "heavenly wisdom?"

1.

2.

3.

4.

5.

6.

7.

8.

3. Which of these characteristics would be helpful when dealing with a person who behaves and believes different from you?

About My Father
Kelby Stahl

I'm a sixteen-year-old girl, going into my junior year of high school and living in a single-parent home. It is just my mom and me and our two animals, a dog and a fish. It has just been us for six years and honestly the best six years of our lives. Here is why.

As a young girl who looked up to both parents, I always thought they would be together forever. Until one day in the middle of fifth grade in a brand new school, I read *the note* and knew our family was crushed forever.

I dreadfully counted down the days when mom and I would move in with my grandparents, and my dad would stay in our house. I was devastated. I was losing my dad, my hero, my rock.

As a few months passed, I was getting ready to go into the sixth grade. I was faced with a new school, new friends, and basically a new life. My dad quickly moved twelve hours away from me.

My mom became my best friend, and she was who I learned to always count on. As the years went by, I had minimal contact with my dad and I quickly learned to move on without him. He chose a different woman to be his wife; one with five kids, who he showed more love to than he did me at this point. My dad was no longer a dad, he was someone who I used to know.

As the last six years have passed, I've had four visits with my father, all which resulted in me leaving early, whether it was 24 hours or 6 days. I quickly lost hope and just gave up trying.

I asked God to come into my life, to guide me, to help me, to love me. His love is like no other. He goes above and beyond to love everybody with the same kind of love. God showed me that I had more to look forward to in this life. .

I thank God every day that He gave me the chance to fight back through the rough times and come out stronger. There is nobody who I love more than my mother who is my backbone and my best friend.

Kelby

Fun Facts:

1. My dog is named Sophie, and my fish is named Mr. Sir Finley.
2. I want to be a physical therapist after high school. It will take around 8 years of school and 3 colleges.
3. My favorite Bible verse is "*God is within her, she will not fall*". Psalm 46:5

I have loved you with an everlasting love; I have drawn you with unfailing kindness.
Jeremiah 31:3

1. Who in your life do you feel has failed you (at least at a time), rejected, or abandoned you?

2. As children of God, for how long can we depend on God's love? What are the conditions (What do *we* have to do to earn that love)?

3. When we forget God and neglect showing Him love, how does Jeremiah 31:3 tell us He responds?

When Your Parents Divorce

Hallie Tyler

When I was nine years old, my parents divorced. This is a very young age to experience this kind of situation, and I took it very hard. All of a sudden my dad, who I was used to seeing every single day, was living in our travel trailer at my grandparent's house.

My brother and I would begin staying with my dad every other weekend. This was a huge change for me, and I can't even imagine what my six-year-old brother was going through. We didn't know why we couldn't have our mom and dad at the same time in the same house. Before long, we were meeting our dad's new girlfriend along with her daughter and son, as well as meeting our mom's new boyfriend.

Let me tell you, my dad's girlfriend and I butted heads pretty quickly. I could not stand that my dad was dating and living with someone else, and I acted out. I started to make rude statements towards her, and even though I would get in trouble I still did it. My dad would constantly be irritated with me and didn't understand why I was so angry.

I would cry to my mom and tell her that I never wanted to go over to my dad's again. I resisted this kind of change, and it made me uncomfortable. I absolutely could not wrap my head around the fact that I had to partially live with someone who I disliked at the time.

When I went to middle school, my dad and his girlfriend moved in together. My brother and I started going to our dad's for a week at a time. It got harder, maybe because I was constantly in denial. I constantly prayed and hoped that I could have my parents together again, but I knew it would never happen.

When my dad and his girlfriend got married, things began to change. I started to be friends with my new step sister. My step mom didn't seem that bad anymore once I actually tried to talk to her and do things with her. We started doing things as a FAMILY, and I felt a change of heart in myself. I was once so resistant to change, and now I was taking it well.

By the time I was halfway through high school, I felt like I had a second mom. I can't exactly explain the change of heart I had, but I had to be optimistic so that I wouldn't be miserable anymore. I was too quick to judge my step mom by her initial acts instead of trying to get to know her.

My parent's divorce was devastating for me, but it sparked a new relationship in my life. If I wouldn't have been so stubborn in the beginning, maybe I wouldn't have the relationship I have now with my stepmom. I was resistant to change.

Even though change can seem difficult, and don't get me wrong it is very scary, embrace it. Change can bring new relationships you never thought would ever be possible. I am so happy that I didn't go through this alone, and my brother and I did it together. We always had each other, and now we are better than ever with our second family.

Hallie
Early, Texas

Fun Facts:

1. I'm a college student.
2. I hate sushi.
3. My favorite holiday is Christmas.

And we know that in all things God works for the good of those who love him, who have been called according to his purpose. Romans 8:28

1. This verse tells us that God works for the good. Who does it say God is working things out for?

2. Does this mean we won't struggle or face disappointment? Does it mean that things will turn out like we wished? What does it mean?

3. What did Hallie pray? Did God answer her prayer, giving her what she asked for? Did God still work for Hallie's good even though she didn't get what she asked for? When has God not given you the answer you'd hoped for, but you know he was still *working for your good?*

That Family

My parents drove a tan suburban. As plain as it was, I was sure our less than cool transportation stood out like a sore thumb. This was in the nineties. We weren't *with it* in the eighties either as far as I was concerned.

Besides using Crest instead of Aqua Fresh (all of my friends used Aqua Fresh), my parents were also considerably strict when it came to entertainment and fashion.

We weren't allowed to watch the most popular TV shows. *Three's Company, MASH,* and later the hit show *Friends* weren't acceptable. I could talk about the latest episode of *Hee Haw* Mondays at school, but that would have only further damaged my social life.

My mom *didn't play* when it came to rules about the music we listened to. Our cassette tapes had to be *curse-free,* and the lyrics couldn't talk about bad stuff. She wasn't afraid to toss our tapes in the trash if they didn't pass inspection.

Parachute pants, Johnny Depp looking hats, collared Coca-Cola shirts and miniskirts would have no place in my closet. Could I wear a bikini? Heck no. (I don't think I was allowed to say *heck* either.)

I lived in Iredell, Texas, population 408. Everybody knew everybody (and everybody's business...there wasn't much else to do but nose around). A few of the more exciting things in our town included the corner store, our six-man football team, and the drill team.

My sister was on the drill team, and when I was old enough I wanted to be on it too. The drill team always performed to the latest music hits and wore showstopping white boots with tassels.

Things got a little rocky one fall when new costumes were announced. In addition to the gold fringed skirts they'd be wearing at some games, the drill team would at other times be wearing unitards without any kind of skirt or anything that would cover the silhouette of (you know)...*what your mama gave you.*

My mom wasn't having it. The drill team leaders knew it, and so did everybody else in town. We, at least for a time, were known as the *wet blanket* family in our attempt to ruin the fun. My sister ended up being the one in the drill line wearing shorts over her unitard.

The good news is that I survived. Not only that, I have zero bitterness about the things *I missed out on.* I may have missed out on a friendship or two due to my boring profile and limited exposure to entertainment and fashion. Looking back, I think that's ok.

There will be those who don't welcome these things about you that you can't change. If they don't accept that you're an obedient kid following rules (that you may or may not agree with), they just might not be the best friend material anyway.

If there are things you want to wear, listen to, watch or participate-in and you think your parents won't approve, talk to them. Don't just assume they'd say no and be miffed about it or go behind their back. Their response may surprise you.

Then again, they may say no and give you a good reason for their decision. They may say no without giving a reason (It happens). You won't know until you ask. In the case that they do say no and you're not happy about it, do pray. Ask God to use your obedience for good. He will be faithful.

And one more big tip! NEVER say you won't be that way when you have kids. You learn things as you get older. You learn with maturity to care less about what other people think and to care more about how to take care of your family in a world that throws a lot of crazy stuff at them that they really don't need...*expensive brand names, countless social media apps that allow you to be in everybody's business (and them in yours) and "entertainment" that supports immoral and unecessary ideas...*

Who would've thought? I ended up being the mom who wouldn't let her kids watch Power Rangers, Bratz, or Pretty Little Liars. They're not allowed to dress like sexy divas or listen to hardcore rap. I hope the avoidance of these things will add to their character. If nothing else, I've given them stuff to write about when they get older.

Honor your father and your mother, as the LORD your God has commanded you, so that you may live long and that it may go well with you... Deuteronomy 5:16

1. What haven't you been allowed to do that you thought was unreasonable?

2. What is something you've been made to do by your parents that you haven't felt was fair?

3. What good will come from honoring your parents even when you don't agree?

CHAPTER 3

Your Tribe

You belong to a tribe called your peers. The funny thing is, there will be times you don't feel like you belong. Throughout the seasons of life you will experience plaguing feelings of insecurity, unaware that those around you are fighting a similar battle. You and those around you may experience times when you are struggling to feel loved or accepted. You may question your ability to weather the changes that come at you. Just remember that you're not alone. You're part of a tribe. And you're learning together.

The Girl that Always Had a Guy
Rebecca Mosley

First there was Jacob in elementary, then Joseph, Jimmy, and Eric in middle school, then Trent my freshman and sophomore year. Then my junior and senior year was Christian, and Justin in college. Some relationships lasted a good solid healthy week, and some lasted for years. YEARS!

Ladies, this is what not to do.

Sure, these relationships were fun! I had someone to call and text every day, I got to exchange Christmas presents and receive love notes, and went on some very fun, creative dates!

One time this guy took me on an Easter scavenger hunt that ended with him in this massive mascot bunny costume at a local park. Talk about creativity! And maybe a little embarrassment.

But with every relationship came another heartbreak. Every "*I love you*" ended with a "*this isn't working.*" Every date or hang out was a night missed with friends and family, and every kiss became a further temptation. Every broken relationship was an increase in insecurity, and every bit of hurt developed a lie that God isn't good. Tears upon tears were shed and a pain came that, for a lack of a better word, stinks.

I'll never forget my first real break up. I didn't know how to deal with that type of hurt. After the dreaded conversation happened with this "guy of my dreams," I immediately called my two girlfriends over. As the night of chick flicks, chocolate, and cries progressed into the late evening, I told them they should sleep in my bed since they were the guests, and I'd sleep on the floor. About fifteen minutes in, of a wide awake night, my friends overheard me crying. No one slept on a comfortable mattress that night...

This heartache led into a battle for this guy's attention. Any glance I could get from him became a glimpse of hope we would get back together. Oh, it was pathetic. There were days of panic if he liked someone else. "*But will he choose me?*" I anxiously thought. I would throw myself on this boy. I did all I could to look and act a certain way. Sure, I thankfully held onto my morals, but I lost all belief in myself. I wasted days thinking, even praying, this would get better.

It didn't end. It just became a bigger issue in other relationships. My goal was to never feel that hurt again so I made every relationship an idol. Always holding onto the desire to save myself for marriage, I still crossed lines I never wanted to. I gave myself emotionally to boyfriend after boyfriend thinking, "*maybe this will be different.*" We would talk about our future together and share our deepest feelings.

I would have never admitted it then, but my boyfriends were my first priority. The first person I thought of in the morning, the first person I thought to spend time with when I was free, and the first person I wanted to confide in about, well...everything. There was a brokenness in me that needed a Savior. Real bad.

Thank you, God, for using my choices in dating to draw me back to You. I'm so thankful You never give up on me.

Something was subconsciously instilled in my heart at a young age that having a boyfriend was a goal achieved. Trust me, my resume of broken relationships and a broken heart is no achievement. Although the Lord has been so patient and loving in His pursuit of me, I am still healing and it is no fun. Shame and guilt are real; feelings that are never meant to be a part of our story, but thank God He is bigger!

Rebecca

Fun Facts:

1. Is it weird that I'm 26 and would still choose a fruit roll up for a snack?
2. In high-school my friends and I refrained from the party scene by making music videos or going to Walmart... truly more fun than any party!
3. As a drum major and head twirler I got to dismiss the band every practice. One day my friend and I provided waters for everyone. Before I dismissed them to go home I shared my faith and told them the water was theirs. I heard later a girl was offended by my story and called me arrogant. She said she felt bad for my future husband! Wow! It stung, but it hasn't stopped me from sharing my testimony in hopes that someone will know Jesus.

Teach me your way, LORD, that I may rely on your faithfulness.
Psalm 86:11

1. What was Rebecca hoping for in a guy? Did she find it?

2. Why didn't she find what she was looking for?

3. What did God teach Rebecca about love and loyalty? What is her advice to you as you seek love?

What You Deserve
Jessica Marcantel

I have always been an overachiever and a perfectionist. Grace has been a subject that is hard for me to fully digest. I have made plenty of bad choices. The devil has always tried, and will continue to try, to throw them back in my face, trying to convince me that I am unworthy to be fully forgiven and loved.

I want you to understand that if you believe that Jesus is your Savior, then ALL your sins are forgiven. There is nothing that you have done that cannot be covered by the blood of Jesus. I don't want you to waste any more time thinking that you are unworthy. Don't listen to the devil when he tells you that you are "not good enough" to date a Godly boy.

He's a big fat liar! He only comes to "*steal, kill, and destroy"!* (John 10:10).

You listen to God's voice. He will reveal to you who you are in Him and what you truly deserve. You deserve to date a boy that loves Jesus. I'm not talking about a boy that kind of likes Him, a boy that was baptized at the age of 12 and has never picked up a Bible since, a preacher's son who dreads going to church, or the boy that says he loves Jesus yet acts like he doesn't even know who He is.

I'm talking about a boy that LOVES Jesus… his love for Him is evident in every part of his life. If he does not love and serve Jesus, YOU BETTER RUN FOR THE HILLS!

You deserve a boy who is kind, trustworthy, and patient.

Look for a boy who is a good leader. I talk to women all the time who wish and pray that their husband would be a good spiritual leader in their household. When a husband is not a good leader, the marriage and household tend to crumble much easier under pressure.

You deserve someone who is selfless; capable of putting others above himself. He should be ambitious. He should have plans and expectations for his future.

You deserve a guy that will never pressure you into anything that you don't want to do. If it makes you feel uncomfortable when he tries to kiss you, you tell him. If a boy is trying to convince you to send him inappropriate pictures, do things with him that you don't want to do, or gets mad when you say no, know that he will not love you or respect you in the way you truly deserve.

You deserve to be loved.

"*Love is patient, love is kind. It does not envy, it does not boast, it is not proud. It does not dishonor others, it is not self-seeking, it is not easily angered, it keeps no record of wrongs. Love does not delight in evil but rejoices with the truth. It always protects, always trusts, always hopes, always perseveres.*" 1 Corinthians 13:4-7

If a guy does not show love in these ways, then he is not dating material. There are guys who will be able to love you in this way.

Because we are human, every boy will fail you and make mistakes. Please don't expect them to be absolutely perfect. I just don't want you to settle for a boy who does not resemble Christ.

Boundaries. Every good relationship has them. Think about the boundaries that we set for our best friends. We expect them to keep our secrets, support us, and take up for us. If our friend goes beyond those boundaries, it's hard to consider them a true friend.

What about the boundaries of a parent and child relationship? When I was a child, my mother expected certain things from me. I was to follow her rules, tell her the truth, and be respectful. When I stepped out of those boundaries, it would affect our relationship. BOUNDARIES ARE VERY IMPORTANT!

If you go into a relationship not knowing what and where those boundaries are, the lines WILL get blurry. Have good boundaries set BEFORE going into a relationship. If a boy truly cares for you, he will respect your physical, spiritual, and emotional boundaries. Do not allow a boy to pressure you into saying things or doing things that are not of Jesus. You deserve a boy that will know and respect your boundaries, keeping them even when it is hard.

God is a good Father who loves you with an unimaginable love. He wants what is best for you; what brings Him glory and points others to Him in your life.

He does not want you to date boys that treat you badly, settle for guys who do not love Him, be in a relationship that is not built on the Foundation of Him, or give into the pressures of a boy's requests. There is forgiveness and grace in our mistakes, but He knows that there are always consequences that come from them. He wants us to be in a healthy, respectful relationship that points people to the feet of Christ.

God did not free you from the bondage of sin so that you could become a slave again. He saved you because of His grace and mercy. You are loved. You are forgiven and free. So, live like it and when you're ready, date like it.

Jessica

Fun Facts:

1. I owned a dog that flooded my house by turning the bathroom faucet on and letting it run while we were gone.
2. I once caught a seagull while trying to fish.
3. I fractured my tailbone while ice skating the day before a dance competition.

"*Love is patient, love is kind. It does not envy, it does not boast, it is not proud. It does not dishonor others, it is not self-seeking, it is not easily angered, it keeps no record of wrongs. Love does not delight in evil but rejoices with the truth. It always protects, always trusts, always hopes, always perseveres.*" 1 Corinthians 13:4-7

1. According to 1 Corinthians 4, what is love? (There are 8 qualities mentioned.)

Love …

1.

2.

3.

4.

5.

6.

7.

8.

2. What qualities does 1 Corinthians say are not love? Love doesn't/ isn't…

1.

2.

3.

4.

5.

6.

7.

3. How does the guy you're choosing to be in a relationship with (or wishing to be in a relationship with) measure up?

Don't just pay attention to how *your guy* treats you. Check out how he treats those without many friends and how he treats his mom or little sister or brother. These qualities don't come easily or naturally. A relationship with Christ is necessary in order to be able to show Christlike love. He may be a *nice* guy, but if He doesn't know Jesus, he can't care for you the way God wants you to be cared for.

Boy Crazy
Janaye Boyd

I'm not sure exactly when it started, but I know from around middle school to the moment I met my husband I was boy crazy. (I googled boy crazy to check if I'm using the term properly. The top definition on urban dictionary said...*Overly concerned with having the reputation of being found attractive by boys*.) That sounds about right. At least, that's how it started.

I can remember in middle school gauging my importance on whether I was noticed by a group of cute/popular boys. I seemed to measure my own worth by what they thought of me. Did they turn and look when I walked past their lunch table? Did they notice I wore my tight jeans today?

My desperation for attention later became desperation to be loved. I always had a crush. I probably tried a little too hard. My desperate state must have been noticeable. I was always chasing after some boy's heart. There was always one boy I was currently obsessing over.

Very often I was rejected and felt the sting of that rejection. It was painful. Why wasn't he interested? Why doesn't he like me? Why did he pick her and not me? Why aren't I good enough?

I actually did have several boyfriends (not at the same time). Throughout middle school, high school and college I did actually "catch" a few. I had one serious boyfriend that became heavily involved in drugs. Another that treated me terribly and made me feel I was never good enough. Another that always put himself first. And another that made me feel so confused by our arguments that I couldn't even tell where I stood.

Boys can be confusing. They can say hurtful things they don't even realize we take to heart and carry with us. For a long time I carried that rejection, pain, and misunderstanding. Looking back I am grateful. I am grateful to God for intervening in these relationships. I am grateful to God for loving me so much that he picked me up and moved me out of some very difficult situations.

God saved me when I didn't know I was lost, when I didn't even know I needed to be saved. One by one these relationships ended (not all were bad). I learned exactly what I did not want in a man.

I pray that you don't have to experience being treated badly to realize you deserve better. I pray that you will know your worth and measure it by God's immeasurable love for you. I pray that you will seek fulfillment and love from Christ before you seek it from a boy.

I am now happily married to a beyond amazing husband. I truly believe to my core that he was handpicked by God for me. He is loving, supportive, caring, encouraging and helpful. Most importantly he loves God. He puts God first and leads our family to follow Christ.

I am grateful for my experiences. Yes, there was pain, rejection and a lot of tears, but it helped me grow.

I am confident in who I am and how I deserve to be treated. Each rejection I experienced was God protecting me and holding out for my match. God's timing is always perfect. So, I pray that you would wait. That you would put God first and that you would love yourself. Trust in God and pour out to Him, in prayer, the desires of your heart. He knows us better than we know ourselves. When everything seems confusing and you don't know where to stand…kneel before God, and He will guide you.

Janaye
Wife, mother, child of God

Fun Facts

1. Scary movies stress me out to the point I now refuse to watch them (as well as movies where everything goes wrong). Stresses. Me. Out. I have to leave the room if it's the climax of an action movie.
2. I love to sing, even though I am a truly terrible singer. I didn't even make fourth-grade choir.
3. I need a happy ending. If there is not a happy ending I don't want to read it, hear it or watch it.

In their hearts humans plan their course, but the LORD establishes their steps. Proverbs 16:9

1. What was Janaye's *boy crazy* plan? She had some success. How did the attention she gained from boys affect her?

2. How did the LORD establish her steps? How did he lead her?

3. When has a plan you crafted failed? What did God teach you/ How did he guide you?

Being Bullied
Valerie Morton

My experience being bullied began when I was in 5th grade. There was a girl who called me names, made mean faces, and stared at me. She would do these things when no one was looking so that there were no witnesses. This would happen every day.

In 6th grade, bullying would happen almost daily. Two girls would write mean notes about me and then stare and laugh at me as they read them to each other. One of the girls would follow me to my locker and call me names. She also would push me into my locker. These same girls would push me in the lunch line and make faces at me and call me names all day.

Since I was in all the same classes with them, the bullying would last all day long. I would tell the teacher, and she would tell me to sit down and "just do my work." I started to feel like I wasn't as good as everyone else and began to feel bad about myself.

I would try to sit with people at lunch, but no one talked to me, so I would eat by myself at the detention table. I also went to the nurse and counselor a lot. I would have stomach aches and headaches almost every day. My school work became affected because of all the absences from leaving school feeling sick.

I was sad and felt anxious all of the time. After two years of being in bullying situations, my parents decided to homeschool me. I started journaling everything about my feelings. As time passed I began to feel better about myself.

As I look back I can see my emotions and feelings have changed, largely because I wrote out how I felt. Journaling helped me leave those bad feelings in the past and get all those bad thoughts out of my mind. I feel my mind is clearer and I worry less. I am happy now.

Valerie

Fun Facts:

1. My favorite food is my mom's tater tot casserole.
2. My favorite Bible verse is John 3:16
3. My favorite book is *Facing the Giants.*

If possible, so far as it depends on you, live peaceably with all. Romans 12:18-19 (ESV)

1. This verse tells us to *live peaceably with all.* If we do our part, will there always be peace between us and those who we're in conflict with?

2. Even if there's not peace *with* the person we're in conflict with, can we still find peace for ourselves?

3. In Valerie's case, what were the two things that helped her find peace and move forward? What other things might God call you to do to find peace?

Hurting People
Crystal Foxworth

There is something I hardly ever think about now, but when I was in 7th grade I could hardly go more than 45 minutes without thinking and worrying about it.

There was a boy I hardly even knew, that for a reason still unknown to me, made up a complete lie about me and told it to his girlfriend. He told her that I was calling him and flirting with him. The only communication we had was at the YMCA. We had said hi to each other.

Because of his lie, she decided to bully me my entire 7th-grade year. I am talking about verbally attacking me. She would wait for me outside of my classroom (after my classes) with her friend that was much larger than me.

She was always harassing me and threatening to beat me up. She even tried a few times, but a teacher would walk up and stop it.

It was definitely a very long, rough year for me. I did tell my parents about it, and they went to the school. I don't feel like the school did much to help.

Then there was a dance where she came up and started hitting me from behind. We did end up going to the police about it. She didn't try to fight me again after that, but she and her friend still harassed me.

I just tried to ignore her as best as I could. On the outside it probably looked like it didn't bother me, but on the inside it tore me up.

I am thankful for my parents listening to me and taking action. I'm thankful for my friends who were there for me and stood by me at school. I was grateful that she was a year older than me and was going to the high school the next year. By the time I got to high school, she had dropped out of school.

I think about those of you who are dealing with a bully. The sad thing today is that just because you aren't at the same school anymore doesn't mean it gets any better. With the way social media works now, bullies get to basically follow you home every day and harass you there too.

My suggestion is if you are being bullied on social media, just do the smart thing, as hard as it may be, and take a break from social media so they no longer have the power to try to hurt you.

I think back, and I know that this happening to me did impact who I am. It prepared me for issues that I would go through later in life when, as an adult, someone was making horrible false statements about me. I had to learn to just be who I am and understand that the people who know me would never believe the lies, and that in the end (although we don't know how long that will take), the truth will come out.

Looking back I wish that I would have started praying for the girl that bullied me during my 7th-grade year. Here is what I know now, that I wish I would have known then…

Hurting people are hurt people.

There were probably a lot of things going on in that girl's home life. I don't know for sure, but I believe she was hurt or scared from pain in her own life. It doesn't make what she did to me okay. I wish I would have prayed for her personally, not just that she would be nice, but to truly have prayed for her hurts to be healed and for her to be able to feel Christ's love.

If you are being bullied please don't deal with it alone, share it with your parents or a loved one that will help. Know that it will get better. The world and God are bigger than your bully!

Crystal
Mother of 4

Fun Facts:

1. When I was in 4th grade I got stuck in quicksand type mud with my friend for over five hours, and my parents couldn't find us.
2. I had to have stitches on my tongue after I fell and bit it.
3. When I was younger, I was the only girl on my soccer team.

...But I tell you, love your enemies and pray for those who persecute you... Matthew 5:44

1. Being in the middle of a situation where you are being bullied feels helpless. What good advice does Crystal give regarding social media (What can you do if you are being bullied by text, on Instagram, Twitter or other forms of social media)?

2. Can a person who is truly being bullied take care of the problem by themselves? Who in your life can you talk to if you are being bullied or abused by someone?

3. How does God tell us in Matthew 5:44 to respond to our enemies? Does loving them mean the same as having a friendship/relationship with them?

Controlling Relationships
Anonymous

I have always been a person with a few really close friends, rather than having a big group of friends to hang out with. Going into high school, I was ready to broaden my group of friends and expand my horizons. I still had my close friends but found a new group of friends that had a guy who showed interest in me.

A few months later we started dating. As time went on, I spent less and less time with my friends and more time with his. Occasionally, I would hang out with my friends on the weekends and think to myself that I needed to do this more often. However, every time I went out with my friends, I would have to answer to my boyfriend.

He always had 3 questions for me after I hung out with any of my friends.

1. Did you talk to any guys?
2. Did anyone hit on you?
3. Who all was there?

How I answered these questions resulted in either a satisfactory response or more interrogation and arguments. He was convinced that I would cheat on him (I had no past of cheating and this was actually my first real boyfriend). After a while, I got tired of answering all of the questions anytime I went somewhere. I stopped hanging out with all of my friends and only hung out with him and his group.

As time went on, most of my friends slowly drifted away. They made other friends and the closeness we once shared was gone. He and I dated for over 5 years and towards the end, God began to open my eyes about the unhealthiness of this relationship. After all of those years, I was finally able to start seeing that the decisions he was making had no concern for me.

If he did by chance ask my opinion on a situation, he always did what he wanted despite knowing how I felt. My heart began to see that this was not how I should be treated, and I broke up with him.

Through all of this I had a great youth minister and friend who both saw that it wasn't a Godly relationship and that I deserved better. They both continued to encourage me to come to church (even though I would have to answer to the "three questions" and deal with the harassment pending the results of who I talked to). My friend would also invite me to hang out with his group of friends. I began to see further that the relationship I was in was unhealthy.

The relationship with my boyfriend started out like a fairytale but gradually became like a prison. If you are in a situation like this, know that you can, and should, get out. It may be lonely and not be very easy, but with God you are never alone and all things are possible.

I am reminded of the Samaritan woman who went to the well in the middle of the day when she thought no one would be there. When she got there, Jesus was there waiting for her like he knew she was coming. He is our only source of true hope and the only one that can satisfy our hearts. The woman filled Jesus' cup from the well that day, but Jesus filled her soul from that day forward.

God is waiting for you when you are ready to take that first step my friend. I am praying that you have the courage to take a stand for yourself, that you get support from those around you, and learn what true love is from our Heavenly Father. I pray that is the relationship you choose to focus on, because it is the only one that can provide true joy.

God blessed me greatly, and I can say that I am now married to a man who values me and my relationships with friends. Most of all, my husband loves Jesus with all of his heart.

-Grown Up Village Girl

Fun Facts:

1. None of the foods on my plate can touch.
2. I can burp the ABCs.
3. I don't like the taste or smell of coffee.

Everyone who drinks this water will be thirsty again, but whoever drinks the water I give him will never thirst... John 4:13,14

1. The woman in John 4 had tried to find love she needed in a man. In fact she'd committed to many men trying to find true satisfaction. Jesus knew she hadn't found it. What did he offer her?

2. The writer of this story made every effort to *make her relationship work.* Her effort didn't satisfy her boyfriend, and it didn't bring her happiness either. While being faithful and unselfish are good qualities, what relationship in our life ought to be the most important one, the one we give our heart and whole self to? Will God still love and accept us when we "get it wrong" in our relationship with Him (when we forget to pray, disobey what He has commanded...)?

3. If you *drink the water* Christ offers (accept him as Lord and Savior), what effect can you see that having on your relationship with your friends? The relationship with a boyfriend? Your parents? Will all of your relationships be healthy if you are in relationship with Christ? What will God guide you to do if a relationship is not healthy?

Queen Bee/Toxic Friends
Elizabeth Lott

When I was in middle school, I was part of a "friend circle" that was comprised of eight girls. Within this circle, there was one girl who led the entire group. She wasn't a bully or overtly mean, but she created inner turmoil in a group of 13-year-old girls that we weren't prepared to understand or deal with.

At lunchtime, we were required to reserve a seat beside her WEEKS in advance because one seat was permanently saved for her "best friend," and we were merely alternates for the other seat. I was constantly questioning myself about who I was, what I was wearing, and things I thought I should like because someone said I should. It was exhausting and depressing.

Thankfully, I had a mother who could see the writing on the wall and wisely told me,

"Girls like that will not always stay at the top. Be kind and make other friends. Find friends who bring you joy."

Thankfully, my mother was right. High school brought new schedules, new friends, and an unfortunate downfall for the *Queen Bee.* I remained friendly with everyone in that group, but we drifted as friends do. I was so thankful my mother continually reminded me that real friends lift you up and make you better.

In my adult life, I have met several new *Queen Bees* who are wearing different clothes and discussing different topics at lunch but who make you question yourself and feel lesser than. When I start to feel doubt about who I am as a person or question my choices after interactions with those people, I take a step back and ask myself, *"Is this person lifting me up and challenging me to be better, or are they are trying to make me doubt myself?"* Because those who want to tear you down and cause you to doubt yourself are not your real friends.

Elizabeth

Fun Facts:

1. I love writing thank you notes to people and sending them in the mail.
2. I could eat a What-a-burger Honey Butter Chicken biscuit every day for the rest of my life.
3. I have a stockpile of Bath and Body Works products that could last me about 14 years.

The righteous choose their friends carefully, but the way of the wicked leads them astray. Proverbs 12:26

1. No matter our age, it's easy to flock toward the *flashy friend, the friend with influence.* What characteristics did Elizabeth learn to look for in a friend?

2. What were some characteristics that Elizabeth learned to look out for?

3. Proverbs 12:26 says that *the way of the wicked leads them astray.* How was Elizabeth led astray by the bad qualities in this *friend?* (How did she start to feel about herself?) In what other ways might a companion lead you astray?

Trusting God When Your Friends Don't
Lori Lehrmann

Different.
Not the same.
Opposite.

Have you ever felt different from your friends? Like you are on another planet from them?

You make choices that are different from what others are doing. You make decisions based off of your gut feeling (which can be the Holy Spirit) while others just do what feels good at the time.

You may choose to listen to different music, wear different clothes, talk differently, and go to church instead of sleeping in or doing other things.

Being a Christian and trusting God when your friends don't isn't always easy. In fact, I don't think it's ever really easy, but I can tell you it can be done.

Trusting in God when your friends don't is going to take some work from you. Are you ready? Sure you are. I know you can do this. I believe in you.

You have to know God.

It can't just be the kind of, "yea, I know God. He sent His son to die for me. Blah, blah, blah." I'm talking you need to open your Bible, read more about Him, and ask Him to help you understand what you are reading. You can't share what you do not know. Learn who God is. Study why and how we should pray. I encourage you to get involved in your youth group, which leads me to my next point...

You need to have a friend/group of friends who share your beliefs and faith.

If you have a foundation of friends who do agree with what you believe in and how you are choosing to live as a believer, then it will help when you run into the friend who doesn't share that same belief. Now, this group of believing friends doesn't need to turn into a clique.

You need to invite your unbelieving friends in.

Let them see how trusting God works for you. Share with them how you've seen God working in your life. They may question your choices or beliefs, but you have the proof to back it up. You may want to begin keeping a journal of how God has worked in your life so that you have proof of the things He has done for you.

You have to be careful not to be critical, but share with them in a loving way. It's not a finger-pointing, *"Oh my gosh, why can't you get this"* type of situation. Be open and honest with them, not backing down if they question or make fun of you. Do it all in love. Offer to pray for and with them when a situation comes up in their life that they may be struggling with. Encourage them to pray and share with them how they can pray.

I recently asked one of my high schooler friends, Caitlin, how she continues to trust God when her friends don't, and she said something that was so profound. She said, "*There are a lot of people that don't always turn to praying first when things go wrong, so I try to encourage them to do that because it really does help everything.*" This next part is what really stood out to me.

"People who put everything in God's hands will soon see God's hand in everything."

Ask God for help in trusting in Him and in sharing that trust with those who need it.

Okay, so we ask God for help or for certain situations to come our way, but so often we don't look for those opportunities. So, ask Him and then watch for him to provide you the chance to share with those friends why you trust in Him and why you believe what you believe.

Another one of my high school friends, Kaitlyn, (apparently I really like friends with that name) shared with me about a time when her volleyball team really needed encouragement. Everything was going wrong; they were playing in a gym with no AC (hello, we live in Southeast Texas...it gets H-O-T-T, HOT!!!!!). They lost the first out of three sets, and her teammates were done. They know that Kaitlyn is a Christian, so she saw this as an opportunity to be a leader and a major encouragement to her teammates who were down and ready to give up. She knew God lifts her up when she's down, so she decided to step up and share what Christ does for her every day.

Trusting in God is your personal choice. You will stand out. It's a given. It's how you respond to standing out that will make a difference in the lives of others. We trust in God because we have been taught that He will take our troubles and our pain. We have learned that God is who He says He is. Now we just need to continue sharing that trust with our friends no matter what.

Lori

Fun Facts:

1. I love to surf. I've surfed in some pretty cool places including Wakiki Beach in Oahu, Hawaii, and Dohney State Beach in Dana Point, California.
2. I love weather. I'm a total weather nerd. When a good storm comes our way, I'm constantly checking different radars and websites to find out all the latest. If I could be anything and not fail, I would be a meteorologist.
3. I love Dr. Pepper. Period. End of story.

You are the light of the world. A town built on a hill cannot be hidden. Nor do people light a lamp and put it under a bowl. Instead they put it on its stand, and it gives light to everyone in the house. In the same way, let your light shine before others, that they may see your good deeds and glorify your Father in heaven. Matthew 5:14-16

1. What four pieces of advice does Lori give concerning trusting God when your friends don't?

2. In what ways is it difficult for you to share your faith with your friends and those around you?

3. Why is it important that those around you know about your faith?

Word Vomit

Every summer I avoided Molly like the plague. It wasn't that I didn't like her. Molly was great. It's just that we had only been friends for a week when I spilled *the secret.* Before my *mouth catastrophe*, we'd cruised around Fun Valley (my family's annual vacation spot) on our bikes without a care. Fun Valley was owned by Molly's grandparents.

Me and my permed hair and bird legs felt pretty proud to be hanging out with Molly who was as cute and trendy as I was awkward. The only thing that was more amazing than being Molly's sidekick was getting to talk to her cute and cocky older brother Kyle who noticed I was alive one day.

For whatever reason, Kyle decided to talk to me one afternoon at the arcade (he probably ran out of quarters to play *Centipede* or *Asteroid*). Molly wasn't with me at the moment.

In our *one sentence apiece* conversation he didn't ask me my name and he didn't tell me his. He didn't invite me to get ice cream at the Snack Shack next door. He just asked me what boy from back home his sister liked. Boy howdy, I knew the answer to that question. She'd confided in me and told me the boy's name. I could *easily* fill that request.

Without hesitation I spilled the secret Molly had so carefully entrusted to me. I mean there was always a chance Kyle would keep the secret and not torture his sister mercilessly with that information, right?

In less than five minutes, Molly rode up on her bike. Her feet hadn't stopped pedaling when Kyle yelled out her crush's name while erupting in laughter. There I stood embarrassed for her and ashamed to be me.

Throwing her bike down, Molly ran off in tears. Kyle probably found more quarters and went back into the arcade. I went and hid. Thankfully Fun Valley was big enough to avoid seeing my friend Molly whom I'd outed.

I not only avoided Molly that summer. I would hope not to see her every summer thereafter, even into my adulthood. I knew she must hate me. Every time I'd see her I'd be reminded of what an untrustworthy friend I'd been.

I never apologized to Molly. In time I told myself she'd probably forgotten what happened. She might not even remember who I was. I tried to convince myself that bringing it up so many years later would be unnecessarily uncomfortable.

Last summer, thirty years later, Molly's family sold the resort to new owners. I missed my chance to give her the apology she deserved and the opportunity to set myself free of that guilt and disappointment I carried those years.

So that my *un*friendly behavior might not be in vain, I leave you with a few thoughts on how to handle your word-vomit (those words you aim to keep inside but come spilling out).

1. It's never too late to apologize, until it's too late. You won't know when the opportunity has passed, so don't wait too long. (I've made several apologies as an adult for decade-old mistakes. Try not to wait that long.).
2. Be courageous enough to deal with the awkwardness that comes with confronting the person you wronged. Being awkward and doing the right thing is better than being comfortable in your wrongness.
3. Seek God's forgiveness first and ask His help in getting rid of any excuses you might come up with not to apologize.
4. If you've wronged someone don't settle with thinking that if they wronged you too, you're even. Just because you both messed up doesn't remove your need to do the right thing. (Molly did nothing wrong, but I remember plenty of times where a friend and I wronged each other and moved on without trying to correct the damage done).
5. Be gracious if you're the one who's receiving an apology. Even if you no longer trust that person or choose to be close friends with them, accept their apology.
6. Don't give yourself credit for *feeling really bad.* Feeling bad and having remorse are useless without action. Take action and then give yourself grace (forgive yourself).

If we confess our sins, he is faithful and just and will forgive our sins and purify us from all unrighteousness. 1 John 1:9

1. Which number(s) on page 128 do you need to remember when making right something you did that was wrong?

2. Is remorse (feeling bad about what you've done) enough?

3. I missed my opportunity to make things right with Molly. Have I missed out on my opportunity to make things right with God in this or any situation? Who do you need to make things right with?

Keeping it Holy

I can't remember ever having *"the talk"* with my mom. We didn't talk much about private stuff in my house growing up. That's mostly how things worked (or maybe it didn't work) in my generation.

I learned what a jockstrap was my fifth-grade year, though not from very good teachers. (My friends, through lunch table conversation, told me our teacher *Mrs. Jones* was wearing one.) I learned about the stuff you're supposed to do when you get married (and not before then) from movies like *Dirty Dancing* as I hit junior high (or when I watched movies and listened to music at friends' houses who had less strict parents than mine).

Knowing that this is a Christian book you can probably guess that when it comes to your body you're being advised to *keep it holy.* And you'd be right. Though this subject can be tough to talk about, I'm risking going full-out awkward to share a worthy message. Who am I talking to here?

- You, the one who hasn't even had your first kiss yet. (Save that thing for someone special.)
- You, Ms. Will of Steel who said long ago you were going to wait and you're determined you'll keep on waiting until you become Mrs. Whoever. (Stick to that commitment!)
- You, the girl who is thinking about giving in, but so far hasn't. (Stay strong even if you're in the minority amongst your peers.)

- You, who've been taken advantage of. Someone took your choice; they stole something you didn't give away. (You're not responsible or found guilty for what someone else has done to you.)
- And you, the one who made a choice one time (or maybe even many times) to share something sacred, your body. (You aren't ruined. Your opportunity to keep your body holy is not removed. God is in the business of redeeming what is His.)

God wants the same from each of you. He wants you to honor God with your body...

1. Because following His design brings Him glory.
2. Because He knows the turmoil that can come when we make dishonorable choices, and He wants to spare us that pain.

What has happened to you in the past and any choice you have already made doesn't put an end to your chance to choose today. Wherever you are in your journey, God is calling you...

Flee from sexual immorality. All other sins a person commits are outside the body, but whoever sins sexually, sins against their own body. Do you not know that your bodies are temples of the Holy Spirit, who is in you, whom you have received from God? You are not your own; you were bought at a price. Therefore honor God with your bodies. 1 Corinthians 6:18-20

Honoring God by being obedient to Him isn't always easy. Honoring God is *impossible* without a personal relationship with Him. Ask God's help *before* you're tempted and *when* you're feeling tempted. If you have suffered abuse at the hands of someone you trusted, or even a complete stranger, allow God to heal you. He will.

Talk to Him when you need His help to start choosing better after a time of going against His design. Always remember, nothing surprises Him. Nothing is too disappointing or too messy for Him to handle. Just try Him. He's waiting.

No, in all these things we are more than conquerors through him who loved us. For I am sure that neither death nor life, nor angels nor rulers, nor things present nor things to come, nor powers, nor height nor depth, nor anything else in all creation, will be able to separate us from the love of God in Christ Jesus our Lord. Romans 8:37-39 (ESV)

<u>Sexual immorality</u> is the sharing of your body outside of marriage (in many forms including sending nude pictures). God designed the body to be shared in marriage only.

Honoring God with your body requires good boundaries. Which of the following boundaries do you practice?

___I go by a rule to not be alone with my boyfriend.

___My boyfriend and I stay out of each other's bedrooms.

___My boyfriend knows that I am committed to sharing my body only in marriage, and he respects that commitment.

___I'm careful about watching movies and listening to music that glorifies immoral sexual behavior.

___Even though I have not yet felt this temptation, *I pray* that God will help me make honorable decisions concerning my body.

___I pray when I am feeling tempted.

___I have someone who I have asked to be my accountability partner when I am dating. They frequently ask me if I'm keeping good boundaries. I can tell them when I am feeling tempted and ask them to pray for me.

___I don't carry on conversations or spend time with boys who make crude sexual remarks or ask for inappropriate pictures.

___ I don't engage in conversation about sexual matters with those who would encourage promiscuous behavior.

Write down the names of two people (or find two people) who you can count on to pray for you, be in your business, and help keep you on track as you seek to honor God with your body.

CHAPTER 4

Your Village

I don't believe your neighbors are your neighbors by accident, or your teachers, your teachers by chance. God puts people in your life on purpose. There are people all around you who care for you. You're surrounded by people with stories and experiences that you can learn from. These people are your village. Receive them.

Love Grew on Baker Street
Marie Rogers

I was 11 years old when my family (Daddy, Mama, sister and I) moved from Arkansas to Baker Street in Springhill, Louisiana. We moved across the street from Pat Rogers and his family. I thought Pat was the cutest thing I had ever laid eyes on. The first day my sister Peggy and I rode the school bus, Pat asked Peggy how old she was. She said she was 17. He said that's what his brother wanted to know. I asked Pat if he wanted to know how old I was, and he said, "No" and ran off home.

My mother already had 10 children, the youngest was 6 years old when I was born. I am relatively certain I was not part of planned parenthood. We had a home full of love, laughter, and music. Most of my family either played the piano or guitar, and we loved to sing. We had family gatherings not only on holidays but we made up occasions to get together. Most important of all, we were a Christian family and our parents took us to church.

Pat and I lived on a street where there were several kids, and we only lived one-half mile from main street. We loved going to the swimming pool, movies, and the skating rink together. We played outside until it was too dark, or we got called home for supper. It was an ideal time to be growing up in a small town. Even though Pat was a grade ahead of me, we shared a lot of the same friends. He even called himself my big brother.

My Mama and Mrs. Rogers (Pat's mama) were the best of friends and loved doing craft projects together. When my Mama died unexpectedly one and one-half years after we moved to Springhill, all my friends' mothers tried to help me, but Mrs. Rogers was the one who really took over. She had lost her mother when she was only 12, so she had compassion for me. Mrs. Rogers cooked for my daddy and me (my sister had already left home), she helped me with my home economics projects, and even sewed for me.

Pat and I remained the best of friends. When he started asking me on dates I resisted because Pat wasn't a Christian and was a drinker. After a time, I told Pat the man I married would be a Christian and wouldn't drink. He started to attend church with me. Pat gave his life to Christ, quit drinking, and we planned our wedding.

Mrs. Rogers played such a big part in our wedding, making my bridesmaids' hats, my going away outfit, and our wedding cake. She made the comment that she felt she was marrying her own son to her own daughter.

Now more than 55 years later with three children, grandchildren, and even great-grandchildren, I know that when God spoke the world into existence He knew that a little girl named Marie Long and a little boy named Pat Rogers would be married almost 10 years after they met in Springhill, Louisiana. My prayer is that all young people planning to marry will look to God for your future mate and always keep God in your lives and marriage.

Marie

Fun Facts:

1. My nickname is Recie.
2. I was not quite eight years old when I gave my life to Jesus.
3. Pat Rogers was the first boy to kiss me.

Now to him who is able to do immeasurably more than all we ask or imagine, according to his power that is at work within us to him be glory… Ephesians 3:20,21

1. God had a plan for Marie and her family on Baker Street. It included a community and then later, a family. Have you seen God working in your life through a neighbor like Mrs. Rogers? A stranger you just met? Someone else?

2. Marie held off on dating her life-long crush because she knew what God wanted her to have in a mate. Can you think of a time when have you given up something you wanted and trusted God?

3. When has God given you something that was more than you could *ask or imagine?* Pray, asking God to help you recognize his *immeasurable* gifts.

Finding My Place
Marshaunna Winston

In my early elementary years I lived in Tacoma, Washington. Tacoma at times felt like a mean place. I didn't have a lot of friends.

Then there was Idaho. I lived there for nine months. I went to school, did my work, and went home.

Next I lived in Oregon. I had a hard time making friends because I moved so much. I also had a skin condition and was made fun of. But in Oregon I had Kylie. She stood up for me when people made remarks. I would try to stand up for myself, but I would get nervous and would start to stutter. If people laughed at me, she would stick up for me. She'd ask them, "*How would you feel if somebody was doing this to you?*"

In fourth grade I learned I would be moving again. I finally had a good friend, but Kylie and I would be living more than a thousand miles apart. Texas was the next stop. Like in other places I didn't make fast friends, but after living in Texas for two weeks I met Ms. Dottie.

She was our neighbor. My grandpa had helped her change some light bulbs, so she had brought us a tray of deviled eggs and sausages. She would often bring us food. My grandpa would treat her neighborly too. He would help with water leaks and other small needs. During a storm one day, my grandpa had me check on her. She offered me a Sprite. That stormy afternoon would be the first time we played board games.

We still play sometimes. Ms. Dottie, with her white hair and glasses, is usually wearing a vest, and she *always* has her hair fixed. She's a small woman, but that doesn't stop her from being competitive. At the top of the scorecard she writes (in cursive) a *"W" and an "L"* for winner and loser. We have to keep track.

I learned quickly that we couldn't play games on Sundays. Ms. Dottie goes to church. I asked her what her church was like. I thought I might want to go. I'd learned about Jesus when I was younger but I didn't completely understand who He was or what He'd done for me. Ms Dottie checked with my mom and then took me to church.

Our timing was great because Vacation Bible School was starting. I saw people from school there. That week I learned that Jesus walked on water. One night Brother Jason, our pastor and Mrs. Kim, our church's children's director came in and shared the message of salvation. I decided to follow Jesus. A month later I was baptized. My mom started coming and was soon was baptized too.

Since then I've become involved in my church. I attend Sunday School and church. I'm a part of an organization called Bible Drill and even competed at the state level. I've learned much of God's word which has helped me grow through troubled times. I'm happier and have a healthier life. I've met new friends through church.

I've since made friends at school too. But I've learned that not all friends have to be my age. Jesus put Ms. Dottie and I together. She's like a grandmother, and she's my friend. When we play games together, sometimes I win, sometimes I lose. But having Ms. Dottie as a friend has been one of my biggest wins.

Marshaunna

Fun Facts:

1. I like Cheerios and peanut butter together. My great grandpa, Grandpa Tom, got me to try them.
2. Once my mom and I had a chance to appear on a Disney Channel show, but we got lost on the way there.
3. I once was so terrified by a snake I ran into the house and locked the door. I had my aunt go with me later to check to see if it was gone. It was still there. It was my brother's toy snake.

"For I know the plans I have for you", declares the LORD, "plans to prosper you and not to harm you, plans to give you hope and a future." Jeremiah 29:11

1. What do you believe was part of God's plan in bringing Marshaunna to Texas?

2. How did God use Ms. Dottie as a part of His plan?

3 Who has God put in your life to help show you God's plans for you? (If you don't know, write a prayer here asking him to put such a person in your life.)

Teacher- Friend or Foe?

Sheila Bass

According to the Merriam-Webster Dictionary, a friend is *"one attached to another by affection or esteem"* or *"one that is not hostile."*

Geez Louise, I would hope that in my 27 years of teaching 5th and 6th-grade students that SOMEONE would've held me in esteem or found me not to be hostile!

Mr. Webster also describes a foe as *"an enemy or opponent."* Granted, on numerous occasions, when I had to practically D-R-A-G classwork out of some students, no doubt I WAS the foe in their minds. Considering these two terms, I suppose a teacher would definitely be considered more of a friend than a foe; but, then, that's totally up to you.

Ahhhh, I can hear those wheels a-turning in your head….How can that be up to ME? Yes, you read it correctly. For the most part, the way you perceive your teacher, or a leader in your life, is based on several factors. True, you're going to get a teacher or two along the way with which you just don't have that connection, no matter how hard you try. For example, my 6th-grade science teacher gave me a 79 on my report card (of course, I EARNED a 79, but that's beside the point). A 79, for crying out loud! Who gives a 79? When my dad looked at my report card, he overlooked all my A's and quickly pointed to my C, "What happened here?"

Well, because of that traumatic experience, I never gave a student a grade that ended in a 9 (unless it was a 99). Yes, all of my former students can thank my 6th-grade science teacher for that little gift. Now let's get on to those measures that you can take to improve your relationship with your teacher.

First of all, you can **be friendly** towards her or him. No, I don't mean like your BFF. Your teachers have friends of their own, so adding you to their lists of friends isn't necessary. Being friendly simply means being kind, smiling, occasionally dishing out a genuine compliment, or volunteering to help them. Using good manners like saying "thank you," "yes ma'am," "no sir," or "good morning" go a really long way in cementing a positive relationship and in setting a good example for your peers.

Another way to ensure you're on an affirmative path with your teacher is to **be interested** in the subject, even if it's not your favorite one. Ask questions, listen when she/he teaches, and have your work completed (you just cannot believe how much this means to your teacher). If you're not doing well in that class, ask if tutoring is offered and then actually GO to tutoring….regularly. To be honest, if a student came to tutoring frequently, I've actually added a few points to the final grade just because of the effort. If a teacher offers extra credit, take it! Even if you think you don't need additional points at the time, do it anyway as a buffer for your final average. When you put forth the effort, the effort always benefits you.

Be kind, show respect, complete your assignments. These aren't only applied to the classroom but to the way we treat all people. Matthew 7:12 says, "*So in everything, do to others what you would have them do to you, for this sums up the Law and the Prophets.*" We also know this as the Golden Rule. It's a standard by which we live that points others to Jesus. Make yourself and Jesus proud.

Retired Teacher
Sheila

Fun Facts:

1. In 1st grade, a runaway neighborhood monkey jumped on my back to get up in our tree in my backyard, giving me deep scratches on my back. Yep, it's true!
2. In 6th grade my best friend threw a rock and hit me on my behind, so I threw a rock back at her and chipped her front tooth. The dentist couldn't repair it until her high school years. Talk about guilt! We're still BFF's to this day...50 years later!
3. My family lived in Northern Ireland in 1983 where my son was born. Beautiful countryside!

"*So in everything, do to others what you would have them do to you, for this sums up the Law and the Prophets.*" Matthew 7:12

1. What are some of the tips Mrs. Bass provides for having a good relationship with a teacher in your life? Would these tips be helpful in your other relationships? In a workplace?

2. If a teacher, or another adult in your life *isn't friendly,* or *doesn't act interested in you,* does that mean you're off the hook from treating them kindly? (What does Matthew 7:12 say?)

3. What other things can you try if you're wanting to improve a relationship you have with an adult at school? At church? In your neighborhood?

The Path of Love
Sara Burt

My 8th-grade year I fell head over heels for a guy. When he showed interest, I was all in. I learned much about myself in that early relationship, primarily that I am fiercely loyal. Many months later when I learned he had cheated, I was devastated.

Rather than reach out to my village of family and friends, I internalized all my brokenness and anger. I used the break-up to puff myself up, telling friends God had bigger plans for me. I portrayed myself as this obedient, God-following young woman while secretly begging God to bring him back to me. I daydreamed incessantly about us reconnecting. He consumed my thoughts, but I did my best to convince those around me I was unscathed.

As the months passed and I kept up the façade, hypocrisy weighed heavy on my heart. My imaginary conversations with myself were self-destructive. Daily I told myself I must not have been "enough" … of something. I appeared a healthy, well-adjusted teenager, but on the inside I was a mess.

About nine months later at church, a friend discovered physical markers on me of my inward turmoil. I convinced my friend what he saw was no big deal. On the way home that night I was proud of my persuasion skills and tried to stifle the nagging fear he might not have bought it.

He didn't.

While sitting in high school biology class several days later, a note from the counselor's office requested my presence. I had this sense something was off. As I turned the office corner, I saw my parents sitting in the office with my school counselor. Evidently, my friend from church had met with his school counselor and shared concerns about my well-being. His counselor called my school counselor, a.k.a. one of my mom's closest friends.

Looking back, life could have gone two different directions as I sat in the office. Recounting my actions over the previous months meant I experienced my parents' and my counselor's grief first-hand. It was brutal. At several difficult moments I wished to shut the meeting down because it hurt so deeply to witness the hurt my actions were causing others. By God's grace, I allowed myself to experience all the ugly feels. I risked allowing people to love me well which meant correcting my behavior and teaching me a different way to react to betrayal and hurt.

The next few years were difficult as I owned my choices. Yes, years. What did I learn? First, I learned that my anger had turned into bitterness and self-loathing. Forgiveness was crucial to move forward. Learning to forgive can be a daily battle. There isn't much glory in it because forgiveness requires mostly sacrifice. Glory is only found in knowing that by rejecting feelings of revenge and self-destructive patterns, we are obeying our Savior. We are trusting His Sovereignty and placing our identity and worth in Him.

Second, I learned while my parents were charged with raising me, I was also responsible for "raising" them. They could not help me if I shut communication down. Not being honest about how I felt meant I couldn't experience the support they could offer either. If you build walls to protect yourself from hurt, those walls also hinder you from experiencing love. God designed our village pathways as two-way streets.

Maybe your situation is different but you find yourself building walls. Reach out to a trusted adult or friend. Your village cannot guide you to restoration if they do not know your brokenness exists. Maybe just as my friend found himself, you are witnessing a behavior that doesn't seem right in a friend. Are you willing to love well and risk friendship as God directs your path?

We never know which path God will have us walk through our village, but if you are a child of God's, rest assured the path you are traveling has a purpose. Open your eyes and love your village well.

Sara

Fun Facts:

1. Two of the three times I broke my arm/wrist, I was roller skating in my driveway. So what was my first job in high school? A DJ and Rink Monitor at a rolling rink, of course!

2. I have a 100% fatality rate with my cats, long before their nine lives were spent. They all dramatically perished in different ways. All freak accidents. Want proof? What cat watches the automatic garage door close on top of itself? Evidently mine.
3. Need to get rid of a rotten pumpkin used for front porch fall décor? Avoid throwing the pumpkin into a pasture with your toy poodle watching. Razzie, my poodle, decided I was offering to play fetch, and she ran to catch the pumpkin quadruple her size. Pumpkin 1. Razzie 0. I do not have much luck with dogs either…

Therefore, my dear brothers and sisters, stand firm. Let nothing move you. Always give yourselves fully to the work of the Lord, because you know that your labor in the Lord is not in vain. 1 Corinthians 15:58

1. Who stood firm for Sara when finding out that she was harming herself?

2. What were some of the positive changes in Sara after her secret pain became known to those who loved and cared for her? What did she learn?

3. In what ways are you ready to stand firm for a friend or loved one who finds herself (or himself) feeling dejected and hopeless?

What "Harvey" Left Behind

Layla Traweek

Tuesday morning the rain came. Hurricane Harvey had already hit parts of Texas, but I was sure it would blow over our area without much consequence. My brother Liam and I sat around in the house while the rain continued to pour throughout the day.

By noon water was standing in the street causing me to look out the front door every thirty minutes or so. Mawmaw had already called and checked on us and my dad (who was stuck at work) had us checking in every little bit to give a report.

Around 5:00 in the afternoon water was creeping up our driveway which meant that the water in the street was at least waist high. We figured at this point we'd be stuck in the house overnight because no truck would be able to make it down our street. We thought about ways to keep water from getting in the house, but what could we do?

By midnight, just as we expected, water started to seep in the backyard and through the garage. It bubbled up through the toilets. We grabbed towels and prayed while we tackled an impossible task. I cried and then moved everything I could to higher ground like the top of my bunk bed.

My Mawmaw had tried to coordinate a boat rescue, but that fell through. She'd decided to come and get us, figuring she'd wade through the river that had formed on Lynwood Lane, our street. (My dad was still flooded in at the hospital.) Fortunately, she met up with two men with a boat who were rescuing others on our street. We waited outside with our bags. Wearing my pajamas and my dad's jacket I was still getting soaked, but I was relieved at the words called out from a stranger on a boat, "Do y'all need help?"

He took us as far as the boat could travel. From there my brother and I waded in water to where my Mawmaw was. I settled in her car exhausted.

Three days later we were able to return to our house, but not to stay. I'd prepared myself for what we might see. Cai my fish survived. The hardest part was seeing my dad broken as he dwelt on not being able to be there with us that night.

Looking back, I was never alone. Not only did my Mawmaw and Dad work to get to us to safety, my friends and I had a group chat going on where we constantly checked on each other through the night, sometimes sending a picture of how high the water was rising. Two of our houses flooded. The other two didn't, but those friends offered to help replace whatever we'd lost.

I'm sitting at three weeks later. I'm still not back in my house yet. People from at least a dozen states are here to help. Everybody from Texas has come together. Tons of people are at church. We realize our need. People continue to offer supplies and even their homes. Even those who have flooded are pitching in, helping tear sheetrock out of houses.

I've lost some things, though not nearly what some have lost. I can say that I've gained some gratitude. I still have a roof over my head. I have my family. And things are slowly returning to normal. So much that this flood has brought in will dissipate, but I hope we won't stop putting our love for others into action. Hurricane Harvey came and went, but it has brought us together. I hope we stay that way.

Layla

Fun Facts:

1. I have brown, curly hair.
2. I love to draw creatures I've invented in my mind.
3. I grow cactus, succulents, and air plants.

Rejoice not over me, O my enemy; when I fall, I shall rise; when I sit in darkness, the LORD will be a light to me. Micah 7:8 (ESV)

1. What did darkness look like to Layla when "Harvey came through"? How do you believe she felt?

2. We all *fall* on hard times. What does Micah say happens for believers after we fall? What do you think it means when it says *I shall rise*?

3. How does Layla say the LORD has been a light in this difficult time?

JV Matters
Hailey Kimler

My freshman year of highschool, I was disappointed. I hadn't made varsity for my school's soccer team. I was told by a lot of people that JV didn't matter, especially for girls. It made me feel inadequate just thinking about it, like I wasn't good enough to try again next year. Especially after seeing the girls from my club soccer team had made it to varsity (It's a long story that I don't have enough space to tell. I'll just say there was already a varsity goalie when I arrived).

But then I met the JV coach. He was blunt and to the point, never really a "feelings" kind of guy. What I did notice was how he believed in us, though. Most JV coaches at other schools didn't care about their team or how they did, but our coach pushed us because he knew we could make it to varsity. I admired how he thought we were more than just JV. It made me want to work hard, so I did.

My sophomore year, I was on JV again, but that time I wasn't disappointed. I was happy, because a lot of the girls from JV last year were on again. I thought of them as sort of my soccer family. We worked extra hard, and we even beat our rival school! We were then co-district champions. Our coach bought us a cake. He made a really long heartfelt speech (I cried, not gonna lie), and he told us he was proud of us. He said he thought of us as daughters.

When he broke the news to us that he was going to work at another school, we were all sad, of course, but we were also happy for him. So, we decided to throw him and his wife a surprise going-away party. The team decided that, as a present, we would all sign a soccer ball saying "Thank you" and give it to him. Needless to say, he was touched by the gesture. (I made sure to give him a bear hug.)

I still look up to him, even though he's now working as a head coach at another school. I'll never forget how he believed in us when no one else did, and how he pushed us to be the best we could be.

A Stressed Student and Meme Lover

Hailey

Fun Facts:

1. I'm actually really scared of zombies. Don't laugh.
2. I want to be an author when I'm older. I've already started a novel.
3. Aliens are real, fight me on this.

As Iron sharpens iron, so one man sharpens another. Proverbs 27:17

1.What did Hailey's coach do that *sharpened* her (helped her grow)?

2. How did Hailey respond?

3. Who in your life has cared for you? Pushed you? Shown you your value?

Girls Around the World

Girls from all over the globe were asked to (in thirty words or less) tell you something they want you to know about life. Here's what they said.

I often think other people have more important and smart things to contribute, but when I say something, people listen and sometimes it seems to take influence.
Eva Jonasson - Sweden

Each person was created unique. There is no need to be jealous or copy anyone. Your life mission is to become the best version of YOURSELF.
Taya Tikhova, 35 - St. Petersburg, Russia

Be like Ruth. "She is clothed in strength and in dignity. She will laugh in the days to come..." Proverbs 31:25 God hasn't designed us to carry fear and worry.
Tammy Hudson, Age 47, Montgomery AL

Be on the right side - your own side. Live in this very (или exact) moment. Always know: you are wonderful! Warm regards,
Yana Novikova-St. Petersburg, Russia

Be somebody that makes everyone else feel like somebody.
Jenna Deupree
Williston, North Dakota

The most crucial thing is not to lose motivation; trusting that you will manage even the very difficult things in life. What doesn't kill you, will make you stronger.
Eva, Czech Republic

Enjoy the simple things that surround us: smiles of other people, sunshine, sunset.
Julia, 37 y.o. Minsk, Belorussia

Be consistent. Be honest to yourself. Accept challenges. Be respectful. Be tolerant to what you see as other people's weaknesses. Love. Let others love you. Love yourself.
Markéta, Czech Republic

Your emotions lie. Learn God's word. Put Him first in everything. Don't stress about the future, trust God to be God. "What if" and "only if" lead nowhere.
Jill Branyon- Nairobi, Kenya

Make good choices. They shape who you will become in life every day. Other people have their own troubles they aren't advertising. A kind word or gesture can brighten someone's day!
Kristen- Alabama

Each of us has some form of beauty. God presented these gifts to us , and it is vitally important that each of us presents that beauty "back" to God.
Ranee Bullard
Evans, Georgia

Be brave. Sometimes it will be hard, sometimes it will be scary. Don't let your fear or the doubts of others hold you back. Work hard and have courage, it's worth it.
Baret Bailey
Illinois

Stay positive, work hard and make it happen, never be afraid to ask questions and when in doubt or worried, pray. Your life is what you make it.
Kaitlyn Kreder
Honolulu, HI

Be strong. Nowhere written does it say that only men can be strong... so trust in yourself and know that you are always stronger than you think.
Jessica Zencey-New Mexico

Kindness matters. Love with your whole heart. Dance always. Sing in your car, loud. Pray. Tell people what they mean to you, now. You are strong, fierce & beautiful.
Debbie Workinger, 38 : Home state, Ohio. Military: Alabama

Don't give advice if nobody asked you about it. Only worry about changing things that are possible to change. Don't live in the past.
Kristina, 30 y.o., St. Petersburg, Russia

Dear young lady, be brave to say the truth here and now. Try not to be a part of silly situations, gossips, intrigues. Then you will have a good conscience. Alina, 23 y.o. Murmansk, Russia

Always remember that things happen for a reason. It's ok to have your moments when you break down, but do not let it define you. Make mistakes. Grow from them. Live your life and enjoy the beauty of becoming.
Mireya Rueda
Stationed in Okinawa Japan

Remember your leaders, those who spoke to you the word of God. Consider the outcome of their way of life, and imitate their faith. Hebrews 13:7

1. Whose advice above can you easily agree with and easily follow?

2. Whose advice is helpful and true, but you find it difficult to practice? Circle three pieces of advice and commit to work on them.

3. What should we look for in those older girls and women around us when seeking wise counsel?

“That a Way E!”
Emily Ancira

When I was 13 years old my dad, my favorite coach, and most importantly my best friend died of stage 4 pancreatic cancer. I was only in the 7th grade. I was old, but not quite mature enough to understand why this would happen to me. I knew and understood that God had a plan; and He did.

I lost my best friend. We did everything together. The reality of not having long car rides anymore from the softball fields was tough to accept. Even though those rides only lasted 15 minutes, it seemed like forever because I had made a few mistakes during our practice and my Dad was going to make sure I knew about it. There weren’t going to be any more “getaway” trips by ourselves. We would not be able to drive through the “Godley lights” because no one would understand like we did.

Now I am 15 years old, more mature than I was when my dad passed. Over the course of the 2-year stretch, I’ve become much wiser and have learned a lot. The whole purpose of me writing this is to share my own experience and life lessons. I’ve learned that EVERYONE goes through a major life-changing experience at some point, whether it be good or bad.

Instead of feeling sorry for myself, I’ve decided to help people that might be struggling with a similar scenario as mine or to provide some encouragement for anyone who is going through a difficult life struggle. Enduring this hardship has enabled me to understand people's pain whenever they go through something life-changing. Although losing my Dad has been difficult for me, on May 28th, 2017, a positive experience changed my perspective.

While on vacation with my mom and sister in San Antonio visiting family, the A&M softball team won super regionals which qualified them to move on to the Women's College World Series. As we're watching the final game in super regionals, we heard the announcer talk about Trinity Harrington's Dad passing away just a week prior to super regionals. Trinity is the starting pitcher for A&M, and I immediately felt a connection to her.

My heart sank, knowing that I had a similar experience as her. I felt like I was back two years ago, when my aunt told me my dad had died. I instantly had this overwhelming feeling inside me. Call me crazy, but I felt an overwhelming urge to attend the World Series and meet her. I put my faith in God to arrange some things for this to happen.

I had a tournament that weekend, which I was pitching in. I didn't want to let my team down by not playing; however, I had been to the doctor for a MRI on my foot and learned that I could not play for several weeks. After receiving news about my foot, I realized that I could possibly attend the World Series. The next step was getting tickets and getting to Oklahoma!

Miraculously, my aunt called telling us that she had already bought tickets for all of us to go watch A&M play in the World Series! I knew right then this was *a God thing.* I wouldn't have missed it for the world. We drove up to Oklahoma City and attended the UCLA vs. A&M game.

Even though they lost, after the game I was able to give Trinity a long note that I had written to encourage her and tell her how proud I was of her for *never giving up* even during hard times. It was the most life-changing experience that I have had, and I was grateful for the opportunity to take a negative situation in my life and turn it into a positive.

You are not alone. No matter your situation, God has a plan for you. You may not understand it now, but as long as you stand by him and have faith, it will all work out. I know my Dad was watching from above saying, "That a way E!"

Emily

Fun Facts:

1. I've played softball since I was 3 (12 years) and I love every minute of it.
2. My favorite color is fuchsia.
3. I LOVE anything with the pattern serape.

So *encourage each other and build each other up, just as you are already doing... 1* Thessalonians 5:11 (NLT)

1. How could you encourage someone who's sick? Who's lonely?

2. It's easy to encourage someone when you yourself are encouraged. When you're discouraged, what are some things you can do to lift your spirits?

3. Like Emily, what painful event in your life could you use to encourage someone else? How would you use that situation to help others?

The Secret of Support
Leigh Karnes

As a middle school student, my home life was drenched in alcohol. Both parents were alcoholics. Of course, I really didn't realize it at first. I just knew that once or twice (or three times in a bad week), my mother would become mean, yell a lot, fall down and often sustain minor cuts or bruises. I recall mostly the shame I felt and the effort with which I went to hide my family life from friends. I rarely invited a friend over, almost never had sleepovers, and tried really hard to keep Mother from going outside on a bad day so neighbors would not see her falling down or hear her yelling.

I remember when we got a second car. My heart broke because then I knew Mother could go to the liquor store any day of the week. Before that, I only had to dread coming home from school on the days she kept the car and drove my Daddy to work. I hated those days because I was pretty sure it would be a bad day.

I was very active in church and participated in most every activity, even youth choir (though I was practically tone deaf). Church was a safe place where I felt loved and accepted. One of my most embarrassing memories occurred when someone from church came to visit my parents and invite them to church. Daddy was not home and Mother had been drinking quite a bit. I was terrified that she would say something insulting, and I quickly excused myself to my bedroom so I would not have to hear what was sure to be an embarrassing exchange.

Though I did all I could do to hide the "family secret," it was inevitable that word would get out in our small community. At church, our youth director was an older (probably 40-45) single lady named Miss Powell. After church one Sunday she asked a classmate, Tommy, and I to represent our youth group at a weekend conference. Of course, we felt honored to be invited, although at age 13-14 it was a little awkward to be traveling on a Greyhound bus with a boy and no adult.

We actually arrived a little late to the opening, and we were not really sure what the theme of the event was supposed to be. By the end of the first evening, I became more and more uneasy because the speakers kept referring to alcohol and how excessive, habitual use affected families. I was thinking, "Is this for me?" Does everyone here know about my family? And what must Tommy be thinking? Or did he have the same problem?

The next day, we were divided into smaller groups where the teens seemed to feel comfortable sharing their thoughts. Several in my group talked about the fear they experienced when their parents drank too much. I was amazed that they felt free to discuss such embarrassing topics. Of course, I never opened my mouth, and I don't recall Tommy speaking either. As the day progressed, I began to hear things like, "*It's not your fault.*" "*You are not to blame.*" "*You can't fix it.*" " *You can learn ways to cope with it.*" I finally understood that this weekend was expressly for children of alcoholic parents. I learned that most of the kids there had experienced the same situations I had experienced, and by talking among themselves they offered support and encouragement to each other.

I learned that alcoholism is a family disease and is often passed down through generations. I learned that children of alcoholics are in every school and though they usually don't talk about it, the effects are always with them. I learned that our youth director knew about my family (and probably Tommy's also) and cared for us enough to "choose" us to attend this conference. Most of all, I was reminded of the love of Christ who intervened through our Youth Director to enable me to learn valuable coping skills in the midst of difficulties.

Years later, as a school nurse in a middle school, I was able to guide other students through similar situations as I facilitated a *Children of Alcoholics* support group. As a middle school student, I couldn't foresee how God would later use my experiences to help other students. Looking back, I see "*the God and Father of our Lord Jesus Christ... who comforts us in all our troubles, so that we can comfort those in any trouble with the comfort we ourselves received from God.*"
2 Corinthians 1:3-4

Leigh

Fun Facts:

1. I have walked a highwire and swung on a trapeze in a circus tent.
2. I can't swim, but I can tread water and doggy paddle.
3. I love to watch British murder mysteries on TV.

Praise be to the God and Father of our Lord Jesus Christ...who comforts us in all our troubles, so that we can comfort those in any trouble with the comfort we ourselves received from God.
2 Corinthians 1:3-4

1. Leigh wanted to keep her trouble a secret. How did this secret affect Leigh's life?

2. How was Miss Powell helpful in the way that she handled the secret she knew about Leigh's family? What did Leigh do later in life that was similar to Miss Powell? (Always be cautious and prayerful with the secrets you've been entrusted with.)

3. Have you ever suffered by keeping a painful secret or shame? What may God eventually call you to do, being that there are those out there suffering alone and in need of comfort?

Find a Mentor, But…
Rebecca Mosley

People are flawed.

What a way to start, eh?

We really are though. It's pretty obvious that we need a Savior. Maybe you're jealous of a friend, idolizing a boy, spending way too much time on your self-image or studies, or fighting with people who are older. Maybe you talk poorly about others rather than encourage. Or maybe you have grown so addicted to technology that you're missing out on true friendships.

All of these examples and the pure fact you are human are motivators to get a mentor.

A mentor is defined as an experienced and trusted adviser. A mentor is also usually

- Someone older, who has experienced life and its milestones a couple steps ahead of you.
- This person takes time to know you.
- They are able to biblically guide the situations, the sin patterns, doubts, insecurities, and life's ups and downs that you face.

They know that you have a science quiz you're nervous about passing, and they know how physical you may have gotten with your boyfriend. They know if you're spending time with the Lord or too much time on social media. They know your favorite restaurant and how to guide the fight you had with your friend last week. This relationship is biblical, and God encourages us to have mentors! They provide opportunity for us to learn how to be wise women who love the Lord!

I have had numerous mentors throughout my life. One in particular knew me and I loved her dearly. I noticed her passion for Christ, and I wanted the same. We had the best talks. She always encouraged me, spurred me on to make wise choices, and spent time with me.

Something changed over time though. I remember hearing she and her husband decided to divorce. I was truly heart broken. I felt involved and responsible to help fix this since I loved my mentor, her family, and I looked up to them.

How could this happen? How could they do this? Aren't they Christians? Don't they know this is wrong? God, can't you fix this?

These thoughts, and more, flooded my mind. I was discouraged and hurt but had no idea that this would be an opportunity the Lord would use to change my heart.

I struggled hard through this. I developed a fear that my husband and I would one day divorce, and I'm not even married! I felt stuck in sadness that God would allow this to happen. I felt discouraged that a Christian marriage had fallen apart and wondered where God was through it all. Over time God was sweet to show me that I had put too much faith in His people and not in Him.

Mentors are necessary. They teach us from their mistakes and encourage us to live wisely, but always keep in mind, they are flawed. A mentor is to be an example, but not our ultimate. God is perfection, a human can never be. I pray this does not discourage you from finding a mentor, but reminds you to put your faith in the One who is our one and only perfect example. If you are struggling with a mentor, a parent, a teacher, a minister, etc who has done or said anything that has affected you negatively, remind yourself that people are flawed. Give them grace as God has given you and continue growing in Him who makes all things good!

Rebecca Mosley

As it is written: "There is no one righteous, not even one... Romans 3:10

1. What are some of the specific qualities Rebecca mentions should be present in a mentor?

2. Who do you look up to the most? A mentor? A parent? Someone else? Though they're not perfect, is God their guide?

3. What are some Christian responses you can practice when someone you've looked to for wisdom and help (like a mentor or a parent) makes a mistake?

Read God's word and talk to him in prayer. Seek his guidance. It never fails.

What's Your Stink?

For we are the aroma of Christ to God among those who are being saved and among those who are perishing. 2 Corinthians 2:15 (ESV)

I made my way around the classroom sniffing, cautiously, that is... I detected a foul odor and I was going to get to the bottom of it. Teaching first graders, I was familiar with certain smells like a carton of rotten milk in a backpack, the scent of cigarette smoke on clothes, and the thing I smelled daily at 1:50, the *post-P.E.* smell.

This smell was none of those, but I recognized it instantly. It was dog poo. "*Poor soul. They must have stepped in it before they got on the bus,*" I thought. Careful to preserve a sense of dignity, I told the kids that one of them had suffered the misfortune of stepping in mess. Gently I began walking around the room requesting to see the bottom of each shoe. Strangely, with each row of desks, the odor never faded or got stronger. As I inspected shoe number 17, all eyes were on me. "*It's you!*" they announced. There behind me and underneath my teacher-shoe was proof.

Lesson learned. Check yourself.

Mess on our shoe isn't the worst time we give off a bad aroma. Our sin can be an ill-effecting and long-lasting stench in the nostrils of people around us.

So...what's your stink?

Is it the way you treat your mom after you woke up late? The way you talk to your brother when you're irritable or someone else made you mad?

Is it some nasty habit you've convinced yourself is ok, even though God's word leads you to believe otherwise?

Are you apathetic about what is right and wrong (You don't really care!)? Apathy stinks too.

Self smell checks should be a priority. Scripture reading and prayer help us to identify where we stink.

Sometimes our senses are dulled and we don't smell our own stink. Other times we smell an odor but think there's no way it's coming from us.

Once, amongst a group of friends, I witnessed a girl being overly critical of a family member. I cringed as she continued to say awful things. Another friend in the group couldn't keep quiet any longer. With a loving smile she looked at our cranky friend and said, "*You're being awful.*" Instantly the criticism stopped. Our conversation drifted to another more healthful topic. That friend who spoke up *stopped the stink.* Those kinds of friends are hard to come by.

We all need a friend that loves us enough to say "*Hey friend that I love... you've lost it*" or "*Take some time to think about what you're doing*".

Most friends won't be honest with you, maybe afraid you'll get mad at them or get your feelings hurt. Maybe it's because we have acquaintances, but few friends as close as a sister (sisters are awesome at pointing out the necessary).

If you're the friend who needs to be honest with someone you love (about their stink), you may worry that your words will hurt rather than help. You may be concerned that Godly counsel may end in your losing a friend. Maybe you fear that in being a friend who *stops stink,* your own stink will be exposed. (*If you're honest with your friends about your concerns, they'll be more likely to be honest with you about your own poor decisions and attitudes.)*

Oil and perfume make the heart glad, and the sweetness of a friend comes from his earnest counsel. Proverbs 27:9 (ESV)

1. What stink do you have in your life currently that you need to be rid of?

2. What do you do with the stink you're aware of in your life?

___Try to hide it

___Blame it on someone else

___Pray about it, asking God to help you be rid of it

___Ask for friends, parents and mentors to hold you accountable

3. When it comes to friends, are you a stink stopper (Do you tell your friends when they're behaving poorly)? Do you have a stink stopping friend?

CHAPTER 5

Bigger Than That

You were created with purpose. You were gifted with a family. You belong to a generation of your peers. You've been placed in a village of people who care for you and will share their story with you. God has arranged all of this. What's more, He is lovingly involved in it all. He conquered sin for you so that your beautiful, purposeful life can be lived out unashamed and unafraid. In fact, *God so loved the world that He gave His son* for all these people in your path and beyond. We've got to get the word out.

Self Worth
Caitlyn Haynes

Not growing up with a dad is pretty confusing, and growing up with a dad who was your best friend and then having him leave without an explanation is heartbreaking. My dad stopped making effort to see me around my 7th grade year of school. It made me question my self-worth and who I was as a person.

Going into 8th grade, I was really lost. I didn't have a great relationship with my mom, and I started trying to find my worth in boys. I wanted to have love from a guy who would stay, so I started doing anything I could to feel wanted by a boy. No matter what I tried, there was always a hole in my heart, a hole that made me constantly ask myself why wasn't I good enough, why didn't my father love me like a father was supposed to, and if he didn't stay what guy would? This stayed with me most of my 8th-grade year, and going into high school it only got worse.

During my first two years of high school, I snuck around all the time with boys and lied to my parents constantly. I was still looking for someone to fill that void I had in my heart with any kind of love. I was making terrible decisions with guys just because I thought if I didn't do what I thought would make that certain guy happy at the moment, he would leave (and I needed that so-called "love" more than anything).

I knew what I was doing was wrong and I felt guilty for it, but I didn't know how to stop. Doing those things and having the guys still leave made me feel worse about myself and made me feel even more unworthy. I prayed constantly for God to help me see that I didn't need to do that, and that someone would stay around for me and love me for me.

Around the end of the summer going into my junior year, I started feeling God nudging my heart, and at the beginning of my junior year I started taking time for myself, started talking to my mom more instead of keeping things in, and prayed more, asking God to help me see my self-worth. He started to show me that no matter what my father down here did, He, my heavenly father, would never leave. Through all the struggles, mistakes, and tears, He was and will always be there. It opened my eyes, and I started realizing my worth little by little.

Then in the summer going into my senior year, I went through a really bad break up. It started to make those feelings of questioning my self-worth come back, but I kept praying for God to take that away from me, and every day He started to show me that no matter who leaves I am worth more than I'll ever know.

God is the only one who can fill that void in my heart I've had for so many years. Self-worth is an everyday struggle for many people, and I am one of them. Finding myself in God was the best decision I've ever made. Realizing that Jesus died on the cross for MY sins, MINE, makes me realize just how worthy I really am in God's eyes. No matter how bad I think my mistakes and sins are, Jesus took care of all that for me. Realize that God gave His one and only son up just so you and I could be closer to Him. That should always remind you how much He truly loves you and how worthy you truly are no matter what struggles you go through in this world.

Caitlyn
Chilton, Texas

Fun Facts:

1. I love writing poetry.
2. Sunflowers are my all time favorite flower.
3. I play 6 different sports.

But God demonstrates His own love toward us, in that while we were yet sinners, Christ died for us. Romans 5:8

1. In the beginning of Caitlyn's story, what was she searching for?

2. Through failed relationships what did Caitlyn realize?

3. How can we know God loves us?

4. How have you been guilty of trying to let people fill the needs in your life that only God can fill?

(Not) Doing the Math
Taya Tikhova

When I was 13 years old, my parents and I decided that I needed to change schools. We dreamed of me getting into the best school in town, Math Lyceum. It was, without any doubt, such a great opportunity. I was so excited! I did really good in school and had big plans about my future in Math studies. There were several entry steps, including a math exam, ability tests, a personality questionnaire, test lessons, and an individual interview. I showed great results but did not make it to the final stage.

I felt so sad, disappointed, insecure, and tired when I didn't find my name on the list. I felt like a failure, and my dreams were ruined. I entered math class in another school and started to learn English, among other things. English became my hobby. Two years later I won a contest and got a United States grant that allowed me to become an exchange student. It was the beginning of an amazing experience. I stayed in a host family and went to school in Iredell, Texas.

Being an exchange student was fun but also challenging at times. Imagine being a 15-year-old girl from a former Communist country, coming to the United States to live in a family, go to school, make new friends, and speak a foreign language for a year. Moreover, I was in a Senior class so I was younger than other students, and it wasn't always easy for me (and for them). And yes, no e-mails back then, no Skype, and no mobile phones (I am kind of a dinosaur).

My host family supported me a lot during that whole year. I am very grateful to them, and I become more grateful with the years. But I am also grateful to them for one more thing. My American mom and dad invited me to attend church with them. It was First Baptist Church in Iredell, Texas.

I want to mention here that I have considered myself a Christian most of my life, but I can't say I knew the Bible very well or went to church often before I came to the US. It was impossible where I grew up. Thirty-five years ago churches were still destroyed in Russia.

And when I started going to church in Iredell, at first I saw it as a family and social activity. I enjoyed meeting new people and going to church service. I also visited youth group and studied the Bible there. And this is when my spiritual journey really began. I got to participate in church activities like going to a Mexican orphanage. I truly accepted Christ in faith and got baptized on May 16, 1999. My life changed forever.

And now I want to get back to the beginning of my story. It is obvious to me now that God had plans for me back then. When I was extremely discouraged, I couldn't even imagine a great journey ahead of me. Sometimes our failure is just a sign that we are not on a right path (I am not such a good mathematician after all) and something much more important is awaiting.

Love,
Taya
St. Petersburg, Russia

Fun Facts:

1. I am a huge soccer fan.
2. My son, my German nephew, and one of my American nephews were born on the same day but different years. (Love you boys! You melt my heart!)
3. I love travelling on motorcycles with my family. (My dad and my brother own motorcycles.)

You will show me the way of life, granting me the joy of your presence and the pleasures of living with you forever. Psalm 16:11

1. What path did Taya have planned for her life?

2. Besides experiencing America, what *way of life* did God have in mind for her?

3. What experience have you had in life that you at first believed *didn't work out* only to later see that *it did work out?*

Another Family
Lily Duong

All my life, I have had a church influence, but my parents were Buddhists. My parents took me to a Lutheran church from when I was in Pre-K to 5th grade. My parents never went to any of the services, but it was weird because they always donated though. I could never get into Buddhism, and like most stories, I felt something was missing. I stopped going to church because I felt judged, and I had no friends. The adults were nice but I didn't enjoy going to church anymore.

In 6th grade, I moved to Pearland, Texas, where it is roughly 20 minutes away from Houston. I didn't make an effort to find a church, but that summer my friend invited me to go to Vacation Bible School. It was fun, but I ended up moving to Nederland, Texas, so I never got to continue going to church with that friend.

It wasn't until my freshman year where my friend Hallie invited me to church once that I went, and quickly it became a weekly gathering. I had another family. I wanted to go to church every Wednesday and soon even on Sundays.

Even though my mom was cool with me going to church, she was not ok with the idea of me getting baptized. I have always wanted to be baptized, so I thought once I grow up, I would do it. But as time passes, God will answer your prayers.

I had been going to First Baptist church for a year. My sophomore year came and my youth minister Adam had this amazing idea to baptize those who wanted to be baptized on a Wednesday in front of their peers instead of the whole church. I automatically knew "*This is for me, for my relationship with Christ, and for the future.*" This was something I had to do. I signed right up for it.

That day on March 7, 2017, I felt like I was starting fresh, anew. It was also raining (drizzling, but so what). It was even more special.

Even though I took a break, grew tired of God, and doubted Him, He still wanted me. As a matter of fact, He wants everybody no matter what they have done.

Lily

Stressed even more than stressed Asian

Fun Facts:

1. I have been to five countries other than America: Mexico, Canada, Thailand, Vietnam, and Cambodia.
2. I have very chapped lips, and I carry vaseline with me everywhere. My friends even bought vaseline for me for Christmas.
3. My mom thinks that essential oils like Tiger Balm cures everything, but I know it at least helps relieve the itch of insect bites.

And now what are you waiting for? Get up, be baptized and wash your sins away, calling on his name. Acts 22:16

1. Lily says that she went to church in her earlier years. In one church she said she felt judged and lonely. In another church she had fun. What did Lily need to discover she needed most (in addition to a welcome place to worship)?

2. Besides finding that she needed a personal relationship with Jesus, what did the last church provide for Lily?

3. Even though she had originally planned to wait, what command did Lily eagerly follow?

I Get by with a Little Help
Kirsten

The day I had my first suicidal thought will be a day I can never forget. It was raining and I had driven out to my nature getaway, tears staining my cheeks. This heavy weight had been crushing me for so long, and I just couldn't take it anymore. I remember staring out my window and begging God to take my life, because I knew I could never do it myself.

"*Please trade my life for Julie's. Give me the courage to just get out of my car and start walking and never come back.*" I remember thinking who would even miss me and how they would they be better off without me. How I prayed that I would just stop feeling the pain or anything at all.

I was raped when I was 22. I had never felt more violated and disgusted with myself than I did in that moment when I realized what had happened. I felt like something had been stolen from me that I could never get back, I had this stench I could never wash away, I had this darkness snuffing out any light trying to find its way in.

I did everything I could to try and forget about it, to pretend that I was fine. I went to church, spent time with friends, and tried to keep myself distracted as much as possible. Over time the weight of my secret began to suffocate me, and everything I had pushed down to the deepest, darkest part of myself came ripping through and out every pore of my body.

I started to believe that God had turned his back on me, that everyone secretly knew and judged me, that what had happened was my fault, and that I had deserved it. I was convinced that every bad thing happening in my life was God's form of punishment. I ran and hid from God, my family, and my friends. I lashed out at anyone who tried to help. I was so blinded by darkness, that when someone tried to reach out to me, I didn't see their love, I saw only their pity.

One day, I got into a heated argument, and to this day, those words still resound in my head, *"You seriously need help, get on some meds."* It absolutely crushed me. The only thing I heard was that I was broken, something was wrong with me, and in my head all my beliefs were confirmed. I was broken, I was ruined, and I was worthless. The darkness took over and screams tore out of me; I plead with God one last time to end my life, for anything just to end it.

After an hour of trying to talk myself down, I shuffled my music as a distraction, and "*His Daughter*" began to play:

"If there's a God out there
Please hear my prayer.
I'm lost and I'm scared,
And I've got nowhere else to go.
I've come a long, long way.
But I'm not sure I can make it much farther...
So if you're listening, could you give a helping hand.
To your daughter."

(*His Daughter* Molly Kate Kestner)

I had never had anything hit me harder than those words. I sat for a long time with the song on repeat, listening to the words over and over again. The story reached down into a deep part of me that had been dormant, and for the first time in a long time, I felt hope.

I decided to get the help I needed, I knew this person and those thoughts were not me. I began therapy and was diagnosed with Depression and Anxiety. After many months of therapy, nightly 3 a.m. phone calls through panic attacks with my mom and best friend, and much prayer, I slowly began to come back to myself and God.

This is the first time I am sharing my story, and it has been one of the hardest things I have ever brought myself to do. This story has brought back so many painful memories that still make my stomach uneasy, but I know that many of you may be going through the same things that I have, and I want you to know that you aren't alone in your pain.

Every day is still a constant battle with my anxiety. My past still haunts me, and probably always will, but I now know that I have people who love me and support me and a God who will always fight for me. It's not always easy to share your pain or your struggles, but know that your feelings are valid and there is nothing wrong or broken within you.

I believed in the stigma surrounding mental health issues, and hid in my shame and clutched onto the idea that my thoughts and feelings would just go away with time. I could not have been more wrong and almost lost everything. Please know that no matter how alone or helpless you are feeling, there is always someone who loves you, support and help when you need it, and a God fighting for you.

National Suicide Prevention Hotline
1-800-273-8255
https://suicidepreventionlifeline.org/

-Kirsten, The Friend You Never Knew You Had

Fun Facts:

1. I have a cat named Donut.
2. I have traveled to 3 out of the 7 continents, but hope to go to all 7 someday.
3. My favorite author is Leo Tolstoy.

"...he turned to me and heard my cry. He lifted me up out of the slimy pit, out of the mud and the mire; he set my feet on a rock and gave me a firm place to stand. He put a new song in my mouth, a hymn of praise to our God. Many will see and fear and put their trust in the LORD." Psalm 40:1b-3

1. What things did Kirsten try and do to get past the darkness caused by the attack she suffered? Did those attempts help heal her?

2. Her calling out to God wasn't so much one of full trust, but more of a desperate plea. How did God answer her?

3. Rather than ridding her completely of the pain, how is God healing Kirsten? What is He showing her about Himself? About herself?

From Shadows to Sanctuaries
Leanne Todd

The child hid quietly under bar stools. The stale stench of beer soured her surroundings. Her knuckles were a blazing raw pink from nearly constant, incessant biting—self-harm, her childhood pastime. She sat huddled up with tiny knees drawn into her chest. The darkened corner underneath the bar served her purpose quite well. Cloaked in the shadows, she hoped to glean more clues from the cursing screams that had, mercifully, subsided. Her parents' hatred for one another was quite the mystery, one that she was determined to solve. And much like any little spy in a war-torn, enemy nation, she subjected herself to much peril in this self-appointed mission.

Her father, a broken man, stared glass-eyed into space, gently musing some past defeat or failure. But no matter about his surly, withdrawn expression - Daddy was usually a funny drunk.

But this time he had upset her mother - again, somehow - and the woman fired back with a verbal grenade that exploded in mid-air over the child's hiding place. This incited the child to gnawing again, drawing her own blood. "*Never mind*," the usually funny man said quickly under his breath, his face reddened, "*Let it go.*"

That's what would cut the child the most...when the woman would humiliate him.

Soon his hazel gray eyes stared off again into some distant yesterday as a steady gray halo of pipe tobacco circled his temples. He dismounted the bar stool, taking hold of metal crutches that creaked slightly beneath his shifting weight as he headed off to the master bedroom. The ash sweet intoxicating aroma followed him as his only faithful companion.

As soon as the door closed behind him, the child emerged from hiding, tip-toeing in sock feet through the living room. She went unnoticed, hearing the clank of ice cubes against a glass as her mother sipped whiskey in silent victory.

Surely there was a reason for these battle cries and if the child could understand why – perhaps, there was hope she hadn't been the cause. She also reasoned that maybe if she was present, their verbal bashes wouldn't come to physical blows. She would rather stand in harm's way than risk her parents physically hurting one another. It gave the illusion of control. Little did she know, the hurting would happen regardless.

But tonight, she ambled into bed. Tomorrow would be Sunday, and Nancy would be there – bright and early, insisting she come to church. Her new sister-in-law...was RELENTLESS. There was no turning down those beautiful big eyes and open arms that always had a hug for her. If there was one ray of sunshine in the dark place of her childhood, it shone from Nancy. She had only refused one invitation for church. And the sadness that eclipsed those shining eyes broke her little heart.

She didn't really care much for going. It was quite the inconvenient departure from sleeping in on Sundays as was her norm. But to see that disappointment again...after all the loving interest Nancy showed in her -- she just didn't want to be the cause of that again. After all, the only thing Nancy asked for was a couple hours once a week. She could handle that.

Despite all the religious artifacts that adorned her childhood home, she had no working knowledge of the God for Whom her older brother and Nancy went to church. Scattered stories from the Bible lay in her memories as recanted by her maternal grandmother during her pre-school years.

But now, an adolescent, these stories were as distant and foggy as a dream upon the wake. And so all that she was left to assume about God, was that He was distant also. And cold like the inanimate statues that had done NOTHING for her parents. And this gradual death of her tiny soul...it was impending.

But Sunday came. And with it, another invitation. A new young pastor led a heated alter call. She wondered if this God was calling her to go down to the pulpit but stood frozen in the pew. Going down there would be an admission, that nothing in her life was "fine" like she told all the church members. And pride held her in a vice. Suddenly the pastor declared, "*I feel the person You are calling today is a youth, LORD.*"

Really, Padre? She quipped silently to herself, *Well then – male or female?*

The pastor soon closed the service. Her heart sank. She repented softly in her sick heart,

> *I will go down next week, God.*

But curious thing about this God she never knew, He was not in the business of being put off. As she stood on the church steps, she heard her name. It was the pastor. He said, "*Leanne...I felt like you were the person the LORD was calling today. And I just felt that He just wanted me to give you this.*"

It was the New Testament. *How did he know it was me?* But no logical explanation would come. And in his eyes, that love – the same love that poured from Nancy.

So she read. And she realized – Christ. He was not cold or distant, He was not "an artifact." He was real. And if He was real...so must be His Father. In Matthew 10:40 Jesus says, "*He who receives you receives Me, and he who receives Me receives the One Who sent Me.*"

After seeing that Jesus had known her, in all her ignorance and eccentricities, and came to die for her – her, spite her jealousies, her pride that had held her in pew, and a thousand other sins...she eagerly received Him. She drank in the Gospel like water to a thirsting soul. But in reading His Gospels she knew one thing...unlike Nancy, He would not require only a couple hours for once a week. He would require her SOUL. But the good news is this: He deserved it.

-M. Leanne
Fulfilled Wife, Mom, Christian Author and Grown Up Village Girl
Nederland, TX

Fun Facts:

1. I met the love of my life while attending the University of North Texas on scholarship.
2. What did I want to be more than a writer? A mom. We have three children, and one of them has Autism. This is a "fun" fact, because we are not sad. Our faith has made us whole.
3. I am the newly published author of, *"Make Way for Baby!"* It is a collection of Christian poetry and prose. The prophet Isaiah and John the Baptist both proclaimed, "*Make straight the way of the LORD."* And "Make Way for Baby!" is about just that. The Baby is the rebirth of the Holy Spirit in our lives and the coming of our LORD.

I have been crucified with Christ and I no longer live, but Christ lives in me. The life I now live in the body, I live by faith in the Son of God, who loved me and gave himself for me. Galatians 2:20

1. What did Nancy do for her sister in law Leanne? What did the pastor do? How do you point others to God?

2. In light of what Christ has done for you, how are you inspired to serve him? To point others to him?

3. When we give our life to Christ we're to be set apart. What might Christ be calling you to give up?

The Letter
Bridget McCarthy

Less than a week after my 11-year old daughter, Avery, died instantly as a result of a car crash, I wanted to run away. I just couldn't be in my house anymore. I was weary of trying to be strong for everyone: for my 3-year old son who kept asking when Avery was coming home; for my 17-year old daughter who was driving the car at the time of the accident and consumed with guilt; for all of Avery's friends who were struggling with how someone they loved could be here one second and gone the next.

I hopped into my car and started driving. I was immediately swarmed by dozens of children dressed in Halloween costumes, laughing and smiling as they went door to door to collect treats. This is so unfair! My daughter should be here! Tears sprang to my eyes so thick I couldn't see. I quickly pulled into a parking lot and started sobbing. Really sobbing. One of those heaving, snot dripping, soul wrecking kinds of sobs.

I started yelling out in my car. I didn't care who could see or who could hear.

"Avery! Help me!" I pleaded. *"Help me! I don't know how to do this! I don't know what to do! Help me, Avery! Show me how to do this!"*

I reached into my purse, searching for a tissue, but my hand pulled out an envelope with my daughter's writing on it. I had totally forgotten about the letter.

Just two weeks earlier I had surprised Avery with concert tickets to see Christian artist Jamie Grace in concert. While we were there, Avery insisted on sponsoring a child through *Food for the Hungry.* I tried to talk her out of it, thinking that a CD or a t-shirt would be much more fun to get. But Avery was relentless. She was not leaving without sponsoring someone. She looked over all the photos of the available children before pointing to a 16-year old girl from Rwanda. "*This one,*" she said simply.

Avery wrote a letter to Alphonsine, our new sponsor child, and asked me to send it. But I didn't have a stamp and it sat in my purse, sealed and ignored, until this moment, when I was screaming out for help in the middle of a parking lot. I carefully opened the envelope and read the precious words my daughter wrote to a stranger:

Dear Alphonsine,

My name is Avery! I am a girl. I live in Wisconsin. I am 11 years old and in the 5th grade. I am here with you always. I will never forget about you. I will keep you in my heart forever.
Do you know Jesus? Because I do and if you don't know him I will share his word with you. I just want to share this verse to you and then I have to go to bed.

Psalm 121 "I lift my eyes to the hills. Where does my help come from? My help comes from the Lord, Maker of Heaven and Earth."

Your sponsor,
Avery

A deep, beautiful peace swept over me, covering me like a warm blanket. Here I had been crying out to Avery for help but this was her way of reminding me that my help needs to come from God. I needed to shift my eyes to Him. And I did. I learned how to cry out to him, scream out my hurt and pain to him, and I learned how to see the beauty and joy he showers me with – even during hard, dark times.

Bridget
Delavan, Wisconsin

Fun Facts:

1. I don't like ice cream.
2. I have celiac disease.
3. I was the lead in the originating cast of *Squirrels in the Attic*, a play written by Pat Lawrence, which means my name is listed in the front of the playbill.

"I lift my eyes to the hills. Where does my help come from? My help comes from the Lord, Maker of Heaven and Earth." Psalm 121:1

1. Bridget's daughter, Avery, wrote a letter. Who all do you believe her words were meant for?

2. Bridget cried out to Avery and Avery answered through the forgotten letter. What profound words did Avery's mom read that pointed her to healing?

3. In what ways thereafter has Bridget learned to ask for help? By *shifting her eyes (turning to God)*, what else is God showing Bridget?

Grease Those Feathers

They were my two roommates, along with my younger sister. They were blue, loud and unbelievably messy.

I used to have two blue parakeets named Jonathan and Jennifer. They were two (of many) pets my parents allowed my siblings and I to have growing up.

I remember that they'd stick their beak in their tail feathers and ruffle it around.

Did they think they were hiding, tucking their head in their behind like that?
Did they have a weird itch?

Nope. They were preening.

As crafty creation would have it, birds (parakeets, ducks, pelicans, osprey etc.) have their own built-in wax/oil gland. The uropygial gland (also known as the preening gland) is found at the base of the tail. *Healthy birds preen* ***daily.*** So in the future, be enlightened when you see a bird stick its beak near its tail. That's a bird that takes care of itself.

After collecting the wax on its beak and head, the bird distributes the wax onto the rest of its body. At the risk of making this sound like a science lesson, I'll tell you a few reasons birds wax themselves.

1. It apparently makes their feathers *more attractive,* thus wooing other birds. The flamingos are "pinker" (and some would say more bright and beautiful) during the season when they preen more often.
2. It *helps keep pests away.* Yay.
3. It *waterproofs* the birds keeping the bird from becoming waterlogged, or weighed down. (That's where the saying "Like water off a duck's back" comes from, meaning that *something is made easier.*)

There's that person we deal with on a daily basis that, for whatever reason, doesn't like us. We're impatient with a family member who means well. We're overwhelmed with things to do like cleaning and getting everything done that's on our list. The day usually holds a thing or two that weighs us down.

Thus the need to wax our feathers.

We all want to be the right kind of attractive (the inner beauty kind). We need protection from pests and we need the kind of spirit that repels the everyday nonsense that gets us discouraged or in a tizzy.

Our *feathers* are waxed when we pray.

I'm not talking the quick thirty-second "Dear God...Amen" kind of prayer. I'm saying we should *keep our minds set on God.* We will be more beautiful in character. He will make us more patient and more forgiving. (Remember that God protects us from some pesky stuff.) For the things we still have to deal with, he'll help remake us so that even those bothersome and hurtful words and events won't stick to us or define us. They'll grow us.

You will keep in perfect peace those whose minds are steadfast, because they trust in you. Isaiah 26:3

1. Name a time that you let something (or someone) *get the best of you.* What happened?

2. How did you respond? How long did you let it bother you?

3. What does God provide that could have helped *grease your feathers* (peace, joy, gentleness)?

Defeating Giants

I've been driving for twenty-seven years, so I guess you could say I'm an experienced driver. That doesn't stop me from being consumed by fear at the thought of driving in certain situations. I'm terrified of driving over bridges. When I'm forced to, the music in the car goes off and no one is allowed to talk so I can grip the wheel and concentrate.. Heavy traffic and overpasses freak me out too. So does driving somewhere unfamiliar, driving someone else's car and driving in rain. Driving is one of my *giants.*

We all face giants; they tower and taunt leaving us feeling hopeless and small.

Though you know God is faithful, you may doubt that he'll bring you through a challenge when you want or how you want.

Feeling inadequate can be a giant in life. Who knew feeling small could be a giant?

Writing an English paper, speaking in front of a group of people, or confronting conflict could be a giant in your life. Giants come in different names and sizes. But I might mention that Goliath, the Philistine giant, told about in the Bible in 1 Samuel 17, is in every way like the giants we face.

Giants press close.

Meanwhile the Philistine, with his shield-bearer in front of him, kept coming closer to David
1 Samuel 17:41

..... *the Philistine moved closer to attack him....*
1 Samuel 17:48

What better way to cause fear? Giants come close. With no regard for safe space, giants inch-in to intimidate. As they become intimate, they know your weak spot and that's where you get hit.

Giants are persistent.

For forty days the Philistine came forward every morning and every evening and took his stand.
1 Samuel 17:16

Goliath, the Philistine champion from Gath, stepped out from his lines and shouted his usual defiance....
1 Samuel 17:23

Those giants we face don't leave without a fight. The giant, worry, may meet you at every corner. Some giants meet you every morning.

Giants aren't easily frightened or phased. Some giants who are temporarily defeated come back, again......and again.

What seems to be a new giant is usually much like an old giant. All giants can be fought in much the same way, as we're told by David:

The Lord who rescued me from the paw of the lion and the paw of the bear will rescue me from the hand of this Philistine."
1 Samuel 17:37

The bad news is: we face the same type of "giant" over and over.

The good news is: We have the same mighty line of defense (God) for each giant and every battle.

Maybe most comforting, **we never face giants alone.**

David's brothers seemed to have forgotten. Sometimes I seem to forget. God won't allow a giant in your midst that he won't help you battle.

Have I not commanded you? Be strong and courageous. Do not be afraid; do not be discouraged, for the LORD your God will be with you wherever you go. Joshua 1:9

1. What are the two bad things about *giants?*

2. Sometimes we can avoid the things that terrify us. Does God call us to face our giants sometimes?

3. What can we remember when facing giants?

Knowledge is Power, but Salvation is Something More

My heart's a big ugly blob without you in it, a four-year-old boy prayed before bed one night.

Even before that, he could answer all the questions asked about becoming a Christian. You've probably heard these questions.

1. What is sin? *Anything we do/or don't do that isn't pleasing to perfect God (the One who created all and knows all things).*
2. Who sins? *Everybody, Romans 3:23 tells us.*
3. What is the penalty (punishment) for sin? *Death. When we die without trusting Jesus, we are separated from Him forever.*
4. What do you believe Jesus did for us? *He willingly died on a cross. He hadn't done anything wrong. Instead He took our punishment (death) upon himself.*
5. Did he stay dead? *No. He rose from the dead three days later.*

Knowing the answers to these questions is important. In fact, your *life* depends on knowing these things. It also depends on a little more than knowledge.

God's dwelling, Heaven, is perfect. It's a place where there's no suffering and no pain. It's a place where love isn't messy or in low supply.

The problem is, we're not perfect and can't do a thing to purchase a ticket to get in. As good as we are at following the rules, hanging out with outcasts, donating to charity and praying, we can't be good enough or do enough good things to earn our place in Heaven. We can't read the book (even if it's the Bible) and pass a test to get in. Our life (with every good act we perform) is still riddled with imperfection and an ugly blob heart.

All of us have become like one who is unclean, and all our righteous acts are like filthy rags… Isaiah 64:6

Being good, no matter how good you are, doesn't eliminate the bad. Enough *good* may hide the *bad.* It may outnumber it, but it doesn't erase it.

You can't add enough sugar (or anything else) to make spoiled milk new. No matter how hard you try, you can't fully fix a broken mirror. You can only stick its brokenness back together.

If you need a glass of milk and the one you have is spoiled, you'll need a new glass of milk. If you long for a mirror that correctly reflects your image, that broken one that has been carefully pieced back together isn't going to do the trick. You need a new mirror.

- We need *to know* who Jesus is.
- We need *to know* we're sinners.
- We need *to receive* a new heart.

Here's where the good news comes in.

And I will give you a new heart, and I will put a new spirit in you. I will take out your stony, stubborn heart and give you a tender, responsive heart.
Ezekiel 36:26 (NLT)

Jesus paid the price for that new heart. He suffered death on a cross so that, upon believing in Him, our sin would be erased and our hearts would become new. Jesus' death covers our sin problem.

Knowing what Jesus has done for us is important, but it's not knowing the answers that creates anything inside us except maybe a knowledge portfolio and then maybe some effort. A new heart and new life can only be given to us through our trust in Christ. Besides knowing that Jesus lived, died, and rose again, we must realize that Jesus did those things for our own personal sin. After understanding that our sin was the reason for his suffering, we have to choose to allow God to take our sinful heart and make it new.

That doesn't mean we don't sin, but sin in its fullness is paid for. We have a place in Heaven and a heart, that though it still sins, wants to please God. We trust God and we ask him to guide us. We learn to be thankful for what he gives and for even those things he takes away. We strive to realize the depth of God's love. And we love him back.

For God so loved the world, that he gave his only Son, that whoever believes in him should not perish but have eternal life. John 3:16

1. What do you need to know about God to become a Christian? Is knowing these things enough?

2. What must you decide to become a child of God (a Christian)? Who should you tell if you make a decision to follow Christ? Besides talking about your decision to follow Jesus, how else can you show the world that Jesus is your Lord?

3. What should your response be for all that God has done for you?

If you have more questions about becoming a Christian find someone who you know follows Christ.

Afterword

Realize those whom God has strategically and lovingly placed in your midst. There are colorful characters with their own *God stories* all around you. Ask them their story. Listen. Lean on them and thank God for them.

One generation commends your works to another, they tell of your mighty acts.
Psalm 145:4

God doesn't write insignificant stories. *Your* story matters. It matters to him and it has purpose in influencing those around you. Trust God. Hand him the pen. What he has planned for you is more incredible than anything you could plan for yourself.

Call to me and I will answer you and tell you great and unsearchable things you do not know. Jeremiah 33:3

Because of God's marvelous plan we courageously and unashamedly carry our scars, thankful for the beauty in what they teach us and what they teach others. We brave the unknown in tomorrow. It isn't always easy (in fact it hardly ever is).

In the face of all this, like countless girls before us…

Check out *The Village Girl Handbook* on Instagram. We'd love to hear from you on our Facebook page, *The Village Girl Handbook.* Visit and tell us what story touched you. Share your own story of a struggle you've overcome or tell us what you're still struggling with so we can pray for you. Let us know what you'd like to see in volume 3.

Thankful we belong to the same village,

Kristi Burden

Made in the USA
Lexington, KY
16 October 2018